GLOBAL WARMING

GLOBAL WARMING

Personal Solutions for a Healthy Planet

Christopher Spence

First published 2005 by
PALGRAVE MACMILLAN™
175 Fifth Avenue, New York, N.Y. 10010 and
Houndmills, Basingstoke, Hampshire, England RG21 6XS.
Companies and representatives throughout the world.

PALGRAVE MACMILLAN IS THE GLOBAL ACADEMIC IMPRINT OF THE
PALGRAVE MACMILLAN division of St. Martin's Press, LLC and of
Palgrave Macmillan Ltd. Macmillan® is a registered trademark in the
United States, United Kingdom and other countries. Palgrave is a
registered trademark in the European Union and other countries.

ISBN 1-4039-6698-2 hardback

Library of Congress Cataloging-in-Publication Data
Spence, Chris, 1970-
Global warming : personal solutions for a healthy planet / Chris
Spence.
    p.   cm.
  ISBN 1-4039-6698-2
  1. Global warming—Popular works.   I. Title.
QC981.8.G56S64   2005
363.738'748—dc22

2004064919

A catalogue record for this book is available from the British Library.

Design by Letra Libre, Inc.

First edition: July 2005
10 9 8 7 6 5 4 3 2
Printed in the United States of America

To Rose Greenwood

*who taught me that one person
can make a difference*

Contents

LIST OF TABLE AND FIGURES

ACKNOWLEDGMENTS

This book was the result of many people's hard work, commitment and belief. David Pervin, Alan Bradshaw and the team at Palgrave Macmillan provided excellent support, feedback and candid advice for two-and-a-half years. When it came to deadlines, David had an uncanny ability to sense the perfect moment either to apply pressure or give me the space I needed—for which I am truly grateful.

My special thanks to a number of friends who also happen to be fellow climate change experts or environmentalists: Malena Sell, Dr. Peter Doran, Charlotte Salpin, Dr. Lisa Schipper, Dr. Andrey Vavilov, Richard Sherman, Prisna Nuengsigkapian, Dr. Juliette Voinov, Angela Churie, Gerhard Mulder, Paola Bettelli, Dr. Emily Boyd, Dr. Joanna Depledge and the incomparable Langston "Kimo" Goree. Their support, feedback and critique of my work was invaluable. I would like to thank Dr. Pamela Chasek in particular for her encouragement and sage counsel, and also for putting me in contact with the good people at Palgrave.

A sincere thank you is also long overdue to my friends and family who are not privy to the unusual world of climate change science and global diplomacy, but who gamely allowed me to test my work out on the "layperson," and who showed faith in the project. Diane Ormrod, Susie Lomax, Marcela Rojo and Sara Velasquez in particular gave me feedback and encouragement at some key moments. Last but certainly not least, Nicole Eppolito was a tireless source of ideas and input when I was revising the text.

Any errors in this book are the responsibility of the author.

Five Major Myths, Five Key Facts

MYTH #1 Global warming is just a theory. The experts have not made up their minds.

FACT #1 The experts are certain—global warming is happening and we are causing it.

MYTH #2 It is not clear what is happening, or how much the weather will change in the future.

FACT #2 The climate is definitely changing, and the speed of these changes is set to accelerate alarmingly.

MYTH #3 Overall, global warming will not have much of an impact on our planet.

FACT #3 It is already wreaking havoc on many of the world's habitats and could cause mass extinctions on a scale not seen in 63 million years.

MYTH #4 Global warming will not affect me.

FACT #4 You may not realize it, but it already is. Global warming now kills 150,000 people around the world every year. It will soon have a serious impact on you and your family's health and finances.

MYTH #5 There is nothing I can do about it.

FACT #5 The threat of a major disaster can still be averted, but only if individuals, government and big business act now.

A Hot Topic

Tornadoes rip through the heart of downtown Los Angeles, leaving thousands dead and destroying countless homes and apartment blocks. In New York City, massive storms and flash floods paralyze downtown Manhattan. Hundreds perish as giant hailstones the size of footballs batter Tokyo.

Think this sounds like the stuff of fiction? You're right. In June 2004, a Hollywood blockbuster, *The Day After Tomorrow,* showed an apocalyptic vision of a world struck by rapid climate change, a world where no one was safe and disaster could strike at any time.

But if you believe major disasters like this could only happen on the big screen, then you're wrong. Dead wrong. As the list of five key myths and facts on the preceding page makes clear, global warming—or "climate change," as the experts like to call it—is here now, causing wild temperature swings and a dramatic rise in storms, heat waves and other extreme weather events. It may not have deluged New York, but it has already brought catastrophe to millions, killing an estimated 150,000 people around the world each year—the equivalent of 50 terrorist attacks like those of 9/11. Warmer, less predictable weather is bringing new diseases in its wake, too, as well as huge economic costs.

And unlike many of the world's current crop of problems, such as malnutrition in Africa or unrest in the Middle East, this isn't just one of those things that is destined to happen to someone else, someplace else. Already, the United States has been affected. In recent years, the number of extreme weather events has been increasing—a change many experts now attribute to climate change. In August and September 2004, the United States suffered one of its worst hurricane seasons ever. The previous year, it experienced its worst "twister" season, averaging as many as 50 a day at one stage, something the National Weather Service described as "very unusual." The tornadoes killed over 40 Americans and forced President George W. Bush to declare Oklahoma a federal disaster area. New diseases such as West Nile Virus have suddenly appeared and spread rapidly across the country. Meanwhile, across the Atlantic, 20,000 Europeans died in a single month in 2003 as a rash of heat waves sent meteorologists running for their record books. And that's just the beginning.

One day soon, climate change is going to affect you. According to a Pentagon report, the changes resulting from global warming could cause such havoc that they bring our civilization to the brink of anarchy and even nuclear war within 20 years. Britain's chief scientific advisor, Sir David King, has warned that climate change represents a far greater threat to world safety than terrorism. Another British expert, Sir John Houghton, has compared it to a "weapon of mass destruction."

But are Houghton, King and the Pentagon right about the risks of global warming? The short answer is, yes. Climate skeptics are becoming an increasingly endangered species. The vocal minority who deny that global warming is happening is now about as credible as people who still think the Earth is flat or smoking won't damage your health. Twenty years ago, even ten, those arguing against climate change might have had a case. Not any more. In recent years the evidence has accumulated to such an extent that it is hard to argue with, and impossible to ignore. Since the 1990s, the Intergovernmental Panel on Climate Change, the world's leading group of experts, has produced increasingly strong warnings about the dangers of global warming. Almost 2,000 climate specialists signed off on their most recent report, which predicted the greatest, fastest changes yet, and which was based on more compelling science than ever before.

These days, if someone tells you global warming is not happening, then either they're badly mistaken, or they're just plain lying. A number of prominent climate skeptics have turned out to be funded by the oil and coal industry, which is naturally worried about its profit margins. Because oil and coal are two of the main culprits behind global warming, some industry officials don't want to believe the climate is changing. They don't want you to believe it, either. Companies have even hired "experts" to deny there is a problem and to lobby the politicians on Capitol Hill—some of whom have worked in the industry themselves.

Vested interests and political lobbying have slowed down action on the problem. It has also confused the public. In the middle of this political storm where billions of corporate dollars are at stake, Americans have been badly shortchanged when it comes to the truth. While scientific certainty improves by the day, studies show the public is being left out in the cold on what is really going on. Myths and misconceptions have multiplied. Key unanswered questions for most Americans include, What exactly is happening to the climate? How bad can things become? How and when will it affect us? What is being done about it? And how can we help?

This book answers all these questions. It offers a no-nonsense guide to global warming, revealing what's actually happening to our weather and how we can expect it to impact us in every part of our lives and in every part of our nation, as well as in the rest of the world. It exposes the politics behind the problem, revealing who has tried to keep you in the dark about it and which leading politicians have been fiddling while the country starts to burn (and flood, and suffer a multitude of other problems). It also explains why you have every right to be worried about what the experts fear is a disaster waiting to happen.

But in spite of the imminent crisis, there is still hope. Although climate change is already with us, the looming catastrophe can be averted if we act now, and act together. If you want to learn how you can protect yourself and others, or if you dream of a safer world for future generations, this book is for you.

CHAPTER ONE

WHAT IS GLOBAL WARMING?

"We know that if climate change is not stopped, all parts of the world will suffer. Some will even be destroyed."

—British Prime Minister Tony Blair, September 2002

Global warming. We've all heard of it. Polls show most of us are concerned about it. If Tony Blair is right, we should be downright terrified. But what exactly is it? Is it natural? Should it be happening? Why is it happening? And what, precisely, is it doing?

You might never have thought so, but Bob Dylan was right; the answer *is* blowing in the wind, or at least, floating in the atmosphere. To understand what's happening with our climate, it's worth bearing in mind that, from a scientific standpoint, you are incredibly lucky to be alive. We all are, actually, and the reason is simple: the planet we inhabit is blessed with some very special conditions that just happen to be perfectly suited to sustain life.

The main cause of this is the Sun, and the heat and light it sends hurtling our way. Seems obvious? Perhaps so, but the irony is that the Sun's energy by itself isn't sufficient to make the planet warm enough for us to live on. Actually, it could easily have been very different here on Earth—and this is where Lady Luck enters the equation.

The reason the Earth is at just the right temperature for humans and other species to develop and thrive is because of a miracle called the "greenhouse effect." It is this phenomenon that keeps temperatures on the Earth's surface averaging a relatively balmy 59°F (15°C). Without it, the mercury would plunge to a rather more bracing 0°F (minus 18°C)—a cold so intense that humanity would never have been able to evolve.

THE GREENHOUSE EFFECT

The greenhouse effect changes the way the Sun impacts the Earth. Like the other planets in our solar system, the energy that the Sun constantly emits strikes our world, warming the surface. Because the Earth is relatively close to the Sun, it receives a fairly large dose of heat—more than, say, Mars or Pluto, which are more distant. But it is not just Earth's distance from the Sun that makes it an ideal breeding ground for life; the size of our planet also makes a difference, with Earth's gravitational pull making it possible for the planet to sustain a relatively thick "atmosphere" around it.

The atmosphere is simply the layer of gases that can surround a planet like a blanket and that is held in place by gravity. Earth does well in this department—better than Mars, for example, which is too small to sustain a life-giving layer. But even if a planet is the correct size to maintain a decent atmosphere, the gases that make up this protective layer might not be the right ones to support life. Venus, for instance, has a thick atmosphere—thicker than Earth's. But its protective layer is composed mostly of carbon dioxide, a gas that traps heat and holds it around the planet. Because it has such high concentrations of this gas, the atmosphere on Venus retains too much of the heat the Sun sends its way—at least as far as humans are concerned. Combined with its closeness to the Sun, the carbon dioxide levels on Venus send temperatures soaring to a toasty 860°F (460°C). No good for us, even if we were just looking for a beachside resort for our summer vacation (we'd be boiled alive).

It is the ability of gases such as carbon dioxide to trap heat that creates the so-called greenhouse effect. The atmosphere of Venus allows the heat of the Sun to strike the planet—just as the Sun's rays enter through a greenhouse's windows and warm the plants within. And like a greenhouse, an atmosphere with carbon dioxide holds on to heat, trapping some of it so that the atmosphere remains warm. Without it, the Sun's energy would just enter the planet, or bounce off it.

In the case of Venus, there is clearly too much heat-trapping carbon dioxide to sustain life. On Earth, though, this heat-trapping gas makes up only a small amount of what's in the atmosphere—

Figure 1.1   The Greenhouse Effect

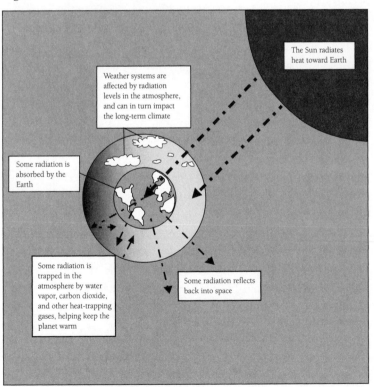

The Sun radiates heat toward Earth

Weather systems are affected by radiation levels in the atmosphere, and can in turn impact the long-term climate

Some radiation is absorbed by the Earth

Some radiation is trapped in the atmosphere by water vapor, carbon dioxide, and other heat-trapping gases, helping keep the planet warm

Some radiation reflects back into space

0.03 percent or so. Nearly four-fifths of our atmosphere is made up of nitrogen, while most of the rest is oxygen. Neither nitrogen nor oxygen traps heat like carbon dioxide does. Even when carbon dioxide is combined with water vapor and the handful of other gases that also trap heat, the levels of these substances are tiny compared to those found around Venus.

For us, though, this is providential. The small levels of heat-trapping gases—or "greenhouse gases"—in Earth's atmosphere are enough to heat up the planet's surface without making it too hot for humans to survive. (See figure 1.1.) Fed by the Sun's warmth, this perfect recipe of atmospheric ingredients keeps our planet at a temperature that's neither too hot nor too cold, but is instead "just right" for humans. Goldilocks would certainly have approved.

But what if the mix changed? What if the amount of heat-trapping water vapor in the atmosphere altered, or the levels of carbon dioxide rose, or fell? Would this influence our climate?

The answer is yes. We all know how fast the weather can change (just ask the good people of San Francisco or London). But it's not just the short-term outlook that can alter; long-term climatic conditions are actually quite unpredictable, too. In fact, the climate has already changed, many times. The fine atmospheric balancing act that makes our world habitable also means it is sensitive to even small changes in the gases that maintain our current temperatures. Put simply, it is easy for our planet to become either too hot or too cold for humanity to thrive.

This has happened on many occasions in the distant past. Scientists believe the climate has changed frequently, even in the past half a million years, which is the mere blink of an eye in our planet's four-and-a-half-billion-year history. There are a variety of reasons for such changes, ranging from slight shifts in the amount of radiation sent our way by the Sun, to the impact of a meteorite hitting Earth.

The experts have labeled such natural changes "climate variability." While it's hardly likely to win any sexy catchphrase competitions, natural climate variability is the reason why our planet periodically heats up or cools down.

But what about now? Can the changes to our climate that most scientists say are happening these days be explained by climate variability? In other words, are the current changes simply par for the course on Planet Earth?

If they were, we would still have plenty of reason to worry. While the last 10,000 years appear to have been relatively stable, scientists believe that, further back still, significant shifts in our weather sometimes occurred rapidly, rather than gradually over centuries or millennia. These changes had a huge impact on animal and plant life, and on entire ecosystems—not to mention on our unfortunate ancestors. Sudden temperature shifts could affect plant and animal life across entire continents, driving species out, or killing them off completely. The onset of, say, a sudden Ice Age could mean that a warmer habitat ideal for lions, crocodiles or gazelles might suddenly be better suited to mammoths, bears or other beasts adapted to live in colder conditions. Alternatively, a climate that suddenly warmed up could have the reverse effect. Conditions for our ancestors could suddenly turn hostile, too, if the weather patterns they were accustomed to changed. As the animals and plants they fed on died out or moved away, our primitive forefathers' survival was threatened as well.

The changes that are happening now are certainly rapid enough to have raised a few eyebrows. In 2001, experts from the Intergovernmental Panel on Climate Change, the leading United Nations body on the science of global warming, confirmed that the 1990s had been the hottest decade since records began 150 years earlier. They also found that average temperatures had risen by roughly 1.1°F (0.6°C) since 1900. While this doesn't sound like much, many experts view it as a shift of seismic proportions, especially as the trend appears to be speeding up. And forecasts for the future are even more alarming. By the end of this century, the Panel expects global average temperatures on the surface of our planet to jump by as much as 10.4°F (5.8°C)—a giant leap over any period.

Worse still, the changes taking place now appear to be almost anything but natural. They could hardly be more *un*natural. According to the vast majority of credible climate specialists, the rapid changes we're experiencing have little to do with nature, and everything to do with . . . us.

VICTIMS OF OUR OWN SUCCESS?

Ironically, the root of the problem lies with humanity's profound success over the last two centuries. Since the start of the Industrial Revolution, our numbers have swelled more than 650 percent, from just 980 million in 1800 to an astonishing 6.5 billion in 2005. We have now explored every corner of the globe, and made massive leaps forward in our understanding of science and nature. We have discovered or invented the internal combustion engine, electricity, mass production, and the microchip. We have unlocked the secrets of the atom, found cures for mass killers like smallpox and the plague, pioneered air travel and manned space flight. What's more, many people (but far from all) have experienced a dramatic rise in their standard of living. The average American factory worker now produces more in a couple of months than his great-great-great-great grandfather could have made in a lifetime's labor. We spend, buy, consume, travel, eat and drink more than ever before. And we live longer. Much longer. The last 200 years have been far and away the most successful period in our history.

One of the biggest (and least well kept) secrets of our success has been fossil fuels. Our innovative ancestors who discovered the benefits of drilling for gas, oil and coal and then burning the stuff to produce energy have helped us blaze a trail from poverty to progress, bringing about the biggest change in our collective material fortunes since our ancestors first climbed down from the trees. Imagine a world without fossil fuels. How would we run our cars, light our homes, power our air conditioners and refrigerators, or play our computers, Playstations, televisions and DVD players? What would we have used to generate electricity in our power plants, run our early steam engines and factories or, later, our airplanes and heavy industries? Some scholars might look back on the pre-industrial eighteenth-century "Enlightenment" period as a cultural revolution. But there was a lot less "light" in the Enlightenment than there is today. It was the Industrial Revolution that brought electric lamps, battery-powered flashlights and a thousand other modern inventions to our homes, shops, streets and workplaces.

The contribution made by oil, gas and coal to our modern lives is incalculable. Even today, when alternative sources of energy have been developed, fossil fuels continue to meet almost all our power needs. Whether it's providing the electricity you need to run your brand new Starbucks-style coffee maker every morning, or the gas to run your car, fossil fuels are still streets ahead of the competition.

Unfortunately, as our economies continue to grow, and as the rest of the world plays catch-up with wealthy countries like the United States, Japan and Britain, we're using more fossil fuels than ever before. Almost four-fifths of the world's energy comes from them. And forecasts suggest their dominance won't end anytime soon, either. On current trends, the world's use of energy is set to almost double in the first 30 years of this century, with about 90 percent of the growth likely to be met by gas, oil and coal. Oil is more in demand than ever, and supplies are expected to jump from 75 to 120 million barrels a day by 2030 (contrary to popular belief, the world's reserves of oil are not going to run out in the near future, and will probably be able to meet growing demand for at least the next three decades, and possibly longer, although prices may continue to rise in tandem with the increased demand). Both oil and coal will maintain their current shares of the total energy market, while natural gas is actually expected to raise its game, grabbing a bigger slice of the pie than ever before. Meanwhile, some alternative sources of energy are expected to go on the back burner. Nuclear power, which now supplies just under 7 percent of the world's energy, is expected to fall back to 4.3 percent, while hydro-electricity will barely hold onto its modest 2.2 percent share. Sources such as solar energy and wind power will grow quickly. The problem is, they currently command such a minuscule share of the market that, unless we change our ways almost overnight, many decades will pass before they make a serious dent in fossil fuels' dominance.

So fossil fuels seem set to remain top dog. But what, exactly, is the big problem with that? Oil, coal and gas have fuelled the human race's rapid march toward progress and prosperity for 200 years. Surely that's a cause for celebration, not concern? Industrialists and business leaders have gloried in the benefits of fossil fuels for a long time. Many still do.

"Oil and gas resources are critical for continuing to improve global standards of living," said ExxonMobil, the world's biggest oil producer, in a recent report on future energy needs.

On many levels, ExxonMobil is right; our world would be far poorer in so many ways without fossil fuels. Technology would never have progressed so far, so fast. But while the triumvirate of oil, gas and coal can be thanked for leading us into the twenty-first century, many now view this "gift" as a poisoned chalice or Trojan Horse. The reason for this is that fossil fuels carry a critical flaw. In the worst case scenario, it could mean that what oil gave us, it could easily take away, sending our civilization crashing down around us.

The problem relates to how oil, gas and coal influence the greenhouse effect. This is because burning fossil fuels to produce the energy to run our cars, homes and offices creates heat-trapping carbon dioxide. Lots of it.

Perhaps you already knew this? What you may not be aware of, though, is just how much of the stuff we've been pumping into our atmosphere.

Since the Industrial Revolution began, our use of oil, coal and gas has been releasing carbon dioxide and other greenhouse gases into the atmosphere in disturbingly large amounts. To give you an idea of just how large, let's start with the average American passenger vehicle. Each year, your car (or SUV, or convertible) probably pumps about five or six *tons* of carbon dioxide out of its exhaust. That's around 11,000 pounds of the greenhouse stuff from just *one* car. Sounds like a lot? Try multiplying it by 542 million—the total number of passenger vehicles in the world today. Now, add hundreds of millions more trucks, motorbikes and other forms of motorized transport. Throw in several hundred thousand power plants, commercial airplanes and diesel-powered trains, millions of factories, tens of millions of offices and billions of homes, all adding to the amount of fossil fuels being burned to produce energy. For good measure, let's toss in the destruction of up to 16 million hectares of forests in the Amazon and other parts of the world every year (trees and plants release carbon dioxide when they die).

The grand total from all this? Twenty-three billion tons each and every year. And counting. Within about 25 years, it will have jumped to 38 billion tons a year. That's almost two trillion tons of carbon dioxide between 1800 and 2030. (See figure 1.2.)

Figure 1.2   Carbon Dioxide Emissions from Oil, Coal and Gas, 1850–2000 (source: IPCC)

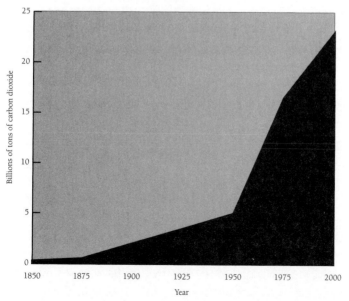

Now, imagine a world without humans. If we weren't here, none of this vast amount of additional carbon dioxide would have been produced. Some would come from trees and plants dying and decaying or from natural forest fires, which release carbon dioxide. More would come from animals breathing (they release carbon dioxide, too, as do humans). Meanwhile at the other end of the line, so to speak, animals' belches and bowel movements release methane, another greenhouse gas, into the atmosphere. Natural disasters such as volcanic eruptions also spew heat-trapping gases. And water vapor in our atmosphere holds onto heat, preventing it from slipping out into space.

But these natural releases of carbon dioxide and other gases have been joined by the huge quantities sent up into the atmosphere by humans. Our use of fossil fuels is responsible for as much as 85 percent of the carbon dioxide that has been added to our atmosphere. And, as if all the carbon dioxide isn't bad enough, we've also managed to increase our use of other greenhouse gases. For instance, our huge increase in population has driven a massive rise in the number of livestock such as sheep and cattle, causing more methane to be unleashed. To top it all, we've even been smart enough to invent some new greenhouse gases all on our own. Some of these, such as halocarbons (which occur only rarely in nature), are far better at trapping heat in the atmosphere than carbon dioxide—although thankfully we do not produce these other heat-trapping gases in such vast quantities. Yet.

PLAYING GOD

"God is dead. . . . We have killed him, you and I," declared Friedrich Nietzsche in 1882. The nineteenth-century nihilist philosopher challenged traditional religious beliefs and sought to place humans at the center of their personal universe. While Nietzsche was certainly not praising our growing tendency to "play God," many writers have since warmed to the idea that we have somehow replaced God on Earth, and are treating the world as our plaything.

Certainly, we have a command and control over our world that no species has had before. But if we have been "playing God," it's clear we haven't always understood the consequences of our games. Never before has a species affected our planet as we have. And never before has a species influenced the atmosphere and the air we breathe like we are doing now. In just 200 years, the mere blink of an eye in Earth's history, we've changed the composition of the atmosphere, adding 30 percent to concentrations of carbon dioxide, doubling the amount of methane, and increasing levels of nitrous oxide (another greenhouse gas) by one-sixth. Researchers believe we've already caused atmospheric concentrations of carbon dioxide to reach their highest levels in at least 420,000 years—and that seems to be a conservative estimate. Possibly, they admit, carbon dioxide concentrations may now be as high as they have been at any time in the past 20 million years. And now, far from slowing down, we're actually spiraling further out of control. Depending on which forecast you believe, sometime in the next 45 to 100 years we'll have managed to double the amount of carbon dioxide in the atmosphere since the Industrial Revolution began. In the name of progress, and quite unwittingly, we've dramatically enhanced the atmosphere's heat-trapping ability. Without knowing it, we've given the Earth a "special power" to hold onto heat that not even a Superman could hope to counter. It is a power that threatens our health, our wealth and our future.

Even two thousand years ago, people saw the dangers of tampering with Nature, of playing God. Horace, a Roman poet, warned that such arrogance could easily come back to haunt us, predicting that if humans pushed their planet too hard, it would eventually push back.

SCIENCE FACT OR SCIENCE FICTION?

But do the warnings about playing God or flying in the face of Nature really apply here? We may know about the greenhouse effect, and the theory that human activities are sending it way out of kilter.

But how certain, really, are the experts about all of this? How sure are they that what we're doing isn't just a drop in the ocean as far as our Earth is concerned? And don't a lot of scientists think our fears about the greenhouse effect and global warming are just hogwash?

Sadly, no. These days, very few experts dispute that climate change is taking place, and that human activities are affecting the climate. Some of the last remaining "standouts" boast some very dubious credentials indeed, and some claim even more doubtful sponsors (see chapter six for more on climate skeptics and the oil lobby). Over the past two decades, a colossal amount of research has gone into the subject. Thousands of scientists and other experts have tackled the issue from many different angles. What is surprising is not the disputes about the science, but the degree of unanimity.

A vast majority of experts are now convinced that climate change is taking place. In 2001, the world's leading body of experts, the Intergovernmental Panel on Climate Change (IPCC), signed off on their latest major document, the 3,000-page *Third Assessment Report*. The Panel made it clear that there is widespread consensus within the scientific community on global warming.

The IPCC's views need to be taken seriously. For a start, it is far and away the world's most respected source of information and analysis on climate change. Founded in 1988 by the World Meteorological Organization and the United Nations Environment Program, the IPCC aims to provide regular assessments of every aspect of climate change, ranging from how and why it is happening, to what has actually changed so far, to what can be expected in the future. The IPCC draws on the expertise of 2,000 recognized climate experts from over 100 countries, who review and evaluate all the latest data, research and findings from the wider scientific community. It is organized into three Working Groups, each of which considers a different part of the climate change dilemma. Working Group I examines the scientific aspects of the climate system and climate change, while Working Group II considers the likely impacts of climate change, and how we can adapt to them. Working Group III analyzes policy options to combat climate change. Every five or six years, the IPCC produces a major report assessing everything we know about climate change, and drawing conclusions on what is really going on. The *First Assessment Report* was produced in 1990, while the most recent, the *Third Assessment Report,* came out in 2001. The next report is expected in 2007.

The certainty of the IPCC's latest report on climate change means something. Scientists are generally a conservative bunch. Remember, their reputations are at stake, which means they're unlikely to say anything they're not 100 percent sure of. Often, they couch their findings and predictions in so many "ifs" and "maybes" that it's hard to read anything into what they say. So, when almost 2,000 experts agree that our emissions of greenhouse gases are affecting the climate, you can believe them. The Panel found "new and stronger evidence" than ever before that most of the warming observed over the past 50 years is caused by human activities. As for the future, the Panel's predictions were considerably more pessimistic than their earlier expectations. The *Second Assessment Report,* published five years before, had forecast that temperatures could rise on average by up to 6.3°F (3.5°C) this century—a worrying enough trend. By the time the *Third Assessment Report* was produced, experts were raising the specter of temperatures climbing far higher—up to 10.4°F (5.8°C). The reason for their change of heart was worrying too: "Confidence in the ability of models to project future climate has increased," they said. What this means is that the computers and other tools they use to forecast how the climate will change have becoming increasingly reliable—and increasingly dire in terms of what they predict will happen next.

So the experts are becoming more certain, not less, about climate change. The question people should be asking these days is not whether it is happening (it is), but whether there is still a credible body of scientific opinion to oppose it. Unfortunately, there isn't. The problem is real, and we need to be prepared.

How Fast, How Furious?

That's not to say there aren't some uncertainties about what will happen, exactly. The computer modeling that simulates future climate change, the extensive data collection and analysis and the other tools used to understand and forecast changes to our climate may be light years ahead of where they were in the 1980s, or even the 1990s. But climate science is an incredibly complex topic. We may have advanced our knowledge in leaps and bounds, but the factors feeding into our climate remain many and varied. Local weather patterns, the interaction between the different gases in our atmosphere, the role played by cloud formations, our oceans and our forests and the atmosphere's ability to cope with change, not to mention uncertainties over what humanity will do from here on in, all make it difficult to predict the future.

This means that, while the experts know climate change is happening, it is not always easy to predict precisely how fast it will happen, and how bad the problem will become. One particular area the experts struggle with is in predicting the localized effects of climate change. While forecasting the big picture globally or regionally is generally more straightforward, drawing that out to predict what will happen in each town or county is another matter. The absence of long-term historical records is a cause of concern, too. Critics worry that we have only been keeping accurate records of weather patterns for 150 years or so—and far less in some parts of the world. In their defense, experts point out that they have been working hard to accumulate more data going back further, with some success. For instance, a team of researchers recently used logbooks from the many British, Dutch, Spanish, French and Portuguese ships that roamed the globe in the seventeenth and eighteenth centuries. Most of these ships kept comprehensive weather readings, and copious records have been preserved from that time to the present day. Experts also employ many other tools to test what the climate was like in the past, from drilling through the ice in polar regions to determine carbon dioxide levels long ago, to studying the development of trees and coral reefs for further clues about how our world is changing.

Another problem for the scientific community is predicting exactly how the Earth will cope with what we're throwing at it. Put simply, we may know the Earth is being affected by what we're doing, but we can't always guess exactly how it will react. Recently, some scientists have warned that the entire climate system could be thrown out of kilter by the massive amounts of carbon dioxide and other gases we're sending up into the atmosphere. According to one theory, this could result in a crisis where the climate system veers out of control, causing it to change in a sudden and dramatic fashion almost without warning. This fear was reflected in the 2004 summer blockbuster *The Day After Tomorrow*. The film drew on theories of abrupt climate change by depicting a climatic Armageddon that certainly made for exciting viewing. Few climate experts would predict such a scenario with any degree of certainty, though. While abrupt climate change cannot be dismissed, we simply don't yet know how close the system might be to hitting such a "critical" threshold.

But even if we dismiss the Hollywood hype, we cannot ignore scientists' warnings that climate change is happening, and threatens us all. The future may or may not look as dramatic as that depicted in *The Day After Tomorrow*, but experts are certain that climate change is with us already, and is only going to get worse. We have every reason to be worried.

DAZED AND CONFUSED?

So the scientific community is now certain that climate change is a major threat. As we've seen, though, this wasn't always the case. It is only during the past 10 to 20 years that the evidence has really stacked up. Until quite recently, debate on the subject has been fierce. In spite of the overwhelming evidence these days, some skeptics still want to argue the point. As you'll discover in chapter six, politicians and big business have been confused (and confusing) on the issue, too.

Under the circumstances, it's hardly surprising that the public hasn't known what to make of it all. A lot of myths and misunderstandings have crept into the picture, making it hard to tell fact from fiction.

One of the worst myths relates to the ozone hole.

THE OZONE MYTH

"Everyone knows the ozone hole is causing global warming," a friend told me over brunch during a recent trip to New York.

"The destruction of the ozone layer is causing more heat to enter into the atmosphere, which in turn is causing global warming, right?" she suggested when I told her about this book and asked her for the lowdown on everything she knew about the problem.

Actually, my friend was wrong, and she's not alone. Surveys show that most people confuse ozone depletion with global warming, or at least believe the two are closely linked. They're not. Global warming and the hole in our ozone layer are two very distinct issues, although you could be forgiven for mistaking the two. Even the media has muddled them up on occasion.

As explained earlier in the chapter, global warming—or climate change—is a result of our ever-increasing use of oil, gas and coal to produce electricity, run our cars and generally keep our modern society ticking. Burning these fuels provides us with energy to keep our air conditioners going or get us to work or school, but they also create carbon dioxide, which is adding to the "greenhouse effect" in our atmosphere. This, in turn, is causing our world to warm up, and our weather to become less predictable and more extreme.

The ozone hole is a different problem. Ozone is a gas that exists in our atmosphere, mostly in the stratosphere, which is about 30 miles above the surface. It forms, disappears and reforms naturally as it interacts with sunlight. Although it can be poisonous to humans up close, ozone forms a natural layer in the stratosphere that actually does a great deal of good. Without it, we might not be here. Unlike low-level ozone, or "smog," which is a far-from-friendly aspect of city living these days, the ozone layer screens out much of the harmful ultraviolet "UV" radiation from the Sun. This radiation is extremely dangerous to us, causing skin cancer, weakening our immune systems and, in some cases, even affecting our eyesight. And it's not just humans who are suffering; ultraviolet radiation can cause serious harm to animals and plants, too. For most of our history we haven't even known it was there, much less what it did. But this hasn't stopped the ozone layer from protecting us against the worst of the UV radiation the Sun sends our way. Until recently, that is.

Experts first started to worry in the 1970s, when researchers with the British Antarctic Survey team discovered something they didn't like at all. Monitoring the atmosphere over the Antarctic, the team detected a dramatic drop in ozone levels in the stratosphere. According to one version of events, the changes were so significant the researchers actually thought their equipment was defective. When it became clear the readings were real, scientists had a lot of work on their hands. For a start, accepted scientific theory suggested the ozone layer should not be changing size in this dramatic fashion.

Scientists also discovered that the thinning of the layer over the Antarctic was no one-off event. As more data was analyzed, it became clear the hole was growing, and was already exposing most of the Antarctic to high levels of UV radiation. On the opposite side of the world, the Arctic was also being affected.

Ozone experts soon discovered the cause. As with global warming, it was something we had brought on ourselves. But the problem this time was not carbon dioxide. Instead, scientists realized the hole was due mostly to man-made chemicals known as halocarbons. These included chlorofluorocarbons (CFCs), a gas we had been using in increasing amounts in refrigerators, air conditioners and as a propellant in aerosol spray cans and even asthma inhalers. Unbeknown to us, CFCs had been slowly rising into the stratosphere, where they were being broken down into their component molecules by radiation from the Sun (which is stronger further from the Earth's surface). Some of the molecules they formed, such as chlorine and bromine, were lethal to ozone. They were, quite literally, killing the ozone layer.

Other gases resulting from human activities were affecting the ozone layer, too, including methyl bromide (an insecticide used by farmers) and carbon tetrachloride (which we use in dry cleaning). Ever innovative, our scientists had discovered chemicals, gases and compounds that our entrepreneurs and inventors could use to help make running our homes, offices, factories and transport systems easier. The problem was, no one had realized the alarming side effects some of these chemicals possessed. These ozone-depleting substances were affecting our polar regions the most, largely because of the particular atmospheric conditions there (especially the unusual cloud formations) and because ozone is easier to break down when temperatures are lower. However, as the years progressed, the thinning of the ozone layer became more apparent around the rest of the world, too. With levels of skin cancer and other illnesses on the rise, it had the makings of a major disaster.

So now you know; ozone depletion and climate change are different things altogether. Those of you who'd thought the two were one and the same shouldn't feel too bad, though. Although they are quite separate issues, both relate to our atmosphere, and one problem has the potential to affect the other. In fact, CFCs are not only an ozone-killer; they also trap heat just as carbon dioxide does, although they are not present in the atmosphere in sufficient amounts to be a major problem as far as global warming is concerned. And as with global warming, you'd also have been right if you'd thought ozone depletion was a problem we humans have caused. Just as with climate change, ozone depletion has the potential to put millions of lives at risk.

Unlike global warming, though, some relatively quick "fixes" are available. Because CFCs were being used in relatively few industries (unlike fossil fuels), scientists were able to find other compounds to replace the CFCs—alternatives that wouldn't contribute to the ozone hole. As recognition of the ozone problem grew, governments responded by agreeing on an international treaty to control the use of substances that were depleting the ozone layer. This treaty, which became known as the Montreal Protocol, was signed in 1987. The Protocol set out deadlines for countries to cut back on their use of CFCs and other harmful substances, and even included an agreement that the world's wealthiest countries should help their poorer neighbors in the fight to protect the ozone layer. Major companies also joined the fray, helping develop alternatives to replace CFCs and the other ozone-depleting substances. As a result of this treaty, progress on controlling CFCs and other similar substances has been brisk. Although the ozone hole is actually continuing to grow due to the long life of CFCs that are already present in the atmosphere, experts are now confident we will soon turn the corner. It may take several decades, but if we stick to our promise to restrict the use of ozone-depleting substances, the ozone layer should eventually make a full recovery.

So we're fixing the ozone problem. Surely we can do the same with global warming? We can. But it's important to bear in mind that the ozone dilemma is in many ways a far easier one to deal with than climate change. While CFCs are used in only a few industries, this chapter has shown that carbon dioxide and other greenhouse gases result from almost every activity humans engage in. Whether we're flicking on a light switch at night or flicking off the alarm clock in the morning, whether we're settling in to watch *CSI* or *ER* on the television, taking a shower, driving to work or flying home to visit the folks for Thanksgiving or Christmas, we're contributing to global warming. It's a monumental problem.

THE END OF THE WORLD IS NIGH!

So is it too late for us? Has our lack of respect for the planet already cast our future in stone? Is spewing out over a trillion tons of carbon dioxide in just two centuries more than the Earth can take? Just what will the consequences be? And is there something we can do to avoid the worst repercussions of our collective excesses?

As you'll see in subsequent chapters, climate change is already with us, and is here to stay. Its effects will be felt everywhere, from our weather (see chapter two), to the world's animal and plant life (chapter three). It is also set to have serious implications for us, particularly in terms of our health and finances (chapter four).

But, there is a solution, a way out. Government and big business must play their part. And we must, too. The second part of this book (chapters five through seven) shows the way forward, and sets out what each of us can do about this titanic problem if we're to avoid going under.

But before we get ahead of ourselves, we need to know just what we can expect climate change to do to our weather.

Chapter Two

What Is Global Warming Doing to Our Weather?

"Millions left without power as Isabel batters U.S," declared America's news anchors on September 19, 2003. Over the previous 24 hours, a powerful hurricane had made landfall in the eastern United States, leaving nearly four million Americans in darkness and without electricity. States of emergency were declared in North Carolina, Delaware, Maryland, Pennsylvania, New Jersey and Virginia. Over 2,000 flights were grounded, and several airports were temporarily closed. At least 15 people were killed. In parts of the Washington, D.C., area, storm surge flooding equaled or exceeded that experienced back in 1933, when the last hurricane of this size had struck. After Isabel had passed, Americans found themselves with a clean-up bill in excess of one billion dollars.

A year later, in August and September 2004, the United States was forced to face something even worse. Four hurricanes struck the country in rapid succession. One of them, Hurricane Ivan, left over 100 people dead in the United States and countries of the Caribbean. Together, the four hurricanes, Charley, Frances, Ivan and Jeanne, caused damage estimated in the tens of billions of dollars.

So what has this to do with global warming? Actually, a whole lot. Climate change is already affecting our weather patterns, causing changes in temperature, rain and snowfall, and even sea levels.

It is also making our weather more extreme, increasing the incidence of severe storms, floods and heat waves. It may even be starting to affect the number and intensity of twisters and (you guessed it) hurricanes.

THE STORY SO FAR

As explained in chapter one, humans have been unwittingly contributing to climate change for a long time now. Since the Industrial Revolution, our burning of fossil fuels has sparked a dramatic rise in the amount of heat-trapping carbon dioxide and other gases in our atmosphere. While the consequences for our climate were not immediate, the last 50 years have witnessed the start of an alteration in our long-term weather. In short, climate change has already begun.

You're Getting Warmer . . .

So what has happened so far? For a start, it's getting hot here in our global greenhouse—or at least, in most of it. The average temperature at ground level has risen by about 1.1°F (0.6°C) over the past century, much of it since the mid-1970s. Temperatures in major cities have increased the most, due to the "urban heat island" effect (more on that later). The four hottest years since records began in 1861 have all happened very recently, with 1998, 2002, 2003 and 2004 occupying the top spots.

According to the World Meteorological Organization, 1998 was probably the warmest 12-month period in 1,000 years, with 2002, 2003 and 2004 close behind. The summer of 2003 produced heat waves in Europe that sent the mercury soaring more than 9°F (5°C) above average for several months, and left more than 21,000 people dead. The temperatures broke national seasonal records in several countries. Near-record summer temperatures were also reported in 2003 in China and parts of Russia, as well as in Canada and the United States (including both Alaska and Hawaii).

These changes are having a profound impact on our planet, from rapid melting of the polar ice caps and glaciers as far afield as Chile and Switzerland, to a sea level rise of 8 inches (20 centimeters) and counting (see chapter three for more on this).

. . . or Are You?

Since the 1980s, the central and southeastern United States, along with much of Asia and central Africa, have seen particularly large temperature hikes. The increase in temperatures has been far from uniform, though. In fact, when it comes to global warming, those living on the east coast of the United States seem to have been left out in the cold a little—at least so far. According to one recent study, temperature changes in the eastern United States have not been keeping up with those occurring elsewhere. James Hansen, one of the "grandfathers" of climate change science, believes that, ironically, the eastern United States has been slightly cooled by global warming in other parts of the world. The NASA expert and some other leading scientists have observed that climate change is causing warming over the Pacific Ocean. Because of the interconnected nature of the global weather system, they believe a complex chain of events starting with this warming in the west is causing a flow-on effect of weather patterns across the United States that is leading eventually to the formation of more cloud cover across the eastern seaboard. Because clouds reflect solar radiation back into space, an increase in cloud cover means less radiation may be reaching ground level in this part of the world, which in turns means less of a warming effect. While this increase in cloud cover is unlikely to make a major difference in the long-term given the strength of the worldwide warming trend, it does show just how complex and interconnected the climate system is, and how the overall warming effect can produce some strange local consequences. Parts of the Southern Hemisphere, and particularly Antarctica, do not appear to have been warming up much in recent decades, either.

The Rain in Spain Stays Mainly on the Plain

At least, that's what Eliza Doolittle said in the classic 1964 film version of the musical *My Fair Lady*. But honestly, what would she know now that climate change is here? In the past half century, rainfall patterns have begun to change. Overall, global rainfall has increased slightly. Many places, from Seattle to Sydney, Australia, to parts of Spain, have experienced an increase in precipitation.

But this trend has been extremely erratic, depending on where you live. In spite of the increased rainfall in some places, others have seen a dramatic drop. Globally, the number of droughts and dry spells appears to be on the rise. In the summer of 2002, the worst drought in a generation struck the continental United States, placing half of the country under drought conditions. Wildfires raged over four million acres, twice the average during the previous decade. Water supplies for residential and industrial uses were threatened and lower lake levels caused serious concerns for electricity generation from hydro-electric power plants. The drought persisted into 2003, continuing what was already a five-year dry-spell in some areas. Water shortages also increased the number of wildfires, breaking records in late 2003 for the most costly fires in the country's history. Australia, too, has seen a rise in the devastation caused by seasonal bushfires. Meanwhile, in Africa, recent years have seen droughts become worse, especially in parts of Ethiopia, Eritrea, Botswana, Zimbabwe, Mozambique, South Africa and the Sudan. However, Kenya, Somalia and elsewhere saw the reverse situation, with unseasonably heavy rainfall leading to widespread flooding in early 2003 and some of the wettest weather in over 70 years.

But if some parts of the world are going to receive more rain and others less, doesn't it all even out? Unfortunately, no. In many cases, the regions that will receive less rain than they do now get too little already, while those that already receive a lot could get even more. Does Seattle need more rain than it already has? Do parts of Texas need less? Probably not.

Another problem on the horizon is that those places that experience more rainfall won't necessarily get it in the way they would like. Farmers in some places (such as those in the northwest) might be grateful for more rain at certain times of the growing season. The problem is, the general trend toward more extreme weather means that increases in precipitation in many places will actually involve *fewer* incidences of rainfall, only in larger amounts. Getting dumped on by torrential rain might result in higher average annual rainfall figures, but it hardly helps crops (or commuters, or roads, or railways, or rivers) when they're on the receiving end of more heavy downpours.

In many places, precipitation is likely to increase only in winter and spring (which results in flooding), followed by too little rain in summer (causing droughts). An example of what we might expect in the future occurred recently in Canada. In 2003, British Columbia experienced a problem with drought and wildfires. The immediate threat was headed off by a bout of heavy rainfall, but the solution only served to create another problem. With 18.5 inches (47 centimeters) of rain soaking the province in just a few days, the downpour caused the worst flooding in more than 100 years. This is hardly an ideal scenario, but just another case of the "wrong place, wrong time" consequences of climate change.

Going To Extremes

In recent years, the scientific community has become increasingly concerned about a rise in heavy rainfall and other extreme weather events. Climate change experts now worry that more intense downpours and storms are on the rise, bringing flash flooding and other unwanted changes. Over much of North America and Europe, scientists estimate that "heavy precipitation events" have increased by as much as 4 percent since the 1950s. Doesn't sound like much? It should, especially if you recall that climate change is only just getting started. In Europe, flash floods are on the rise. China and other parts of Asia are likely to experience more flooding, too. In August

2004, flash flooding was simultaneously causing extensive damage in places as far apart as the Philippines, the UK, southwest China, northern India and Bangladesh.

While the jury is still out on how climate change affects hurricanes, some experts now think these phenomena could be increasing, given that hurricanes seem to form more easily in warmer weather. In the Atlantic, there has been a noticeable rise in the number of hurricanes since the mid-1990s. In 2003, 16 major storms were identified, well above the average for 1944–1996, which was just 9.8 per year. In 2003 alone, Hurricane Isabel devastated the eastern United States, while Hurricane Juan was the worst hurricane to have hit Halifax, Nova Scotia, in living memory. Hurricane Fabian, which struck Bermuda, was the most destructive in 75 years. The following year, in August and September 2004, four hurricanes struck the United States one after the other. Hurricane Ivan left over 100 dead in the Caribbean and southeastern United States and damaged 90 percent of all the buildings in Grenada, while Frances and Charley left hundreds of thousands of Americans temporarily homeless and without access to electricity. Meanwhile, the number of tornadoes in the United States has also been on the rise recently, with 300 occurring in a single week in 2003, and 84 recorded on a single day in May 2004. To be fair, many experts remain cautious about reading too much into the rise in hurricanes and twisters, arguing that more time and evidence is needed to confirm these as long-terms trends. They also rightly point out that it is not possible to blame specific storms, tornadoes or similar extreme events on climate change. On the other hand, there is clearly growing evidence for an overall increase in extreme weather phenomena.

Killer heat waves are increasing in frequency as well, with a clear trend toward more extreme temperatures, particularly in the Northern Hemisphere. On the other hand, the number of cold freezes and winter snowstorms has fallen a little, although even here, some places have bucked the trend—for instance, parts of the United States and Canada experienced a particularly bad winter in 2003/2004.

THE FUTURE'S SO HOT!

It certainly is. The models have told us so. Sadly, though, we're not talking about svelte runway professionals giving us the lowdown on next season's fashions. Almost every mainstream computer model and scenario used for predicting the world's future climate has found that global average temperatures will rise. The differences depend mostly on what assumptions the computer models make about what humankind is going to do in the coming years. Given that we've caused the problem, our reaction to it as time goes by will have a huge impact on what we can expect in the future. Scenarios range from those assuming a "business-as-usual" approach where we continue to do things pretty much as we always have, to those that assume we have responded seriously to climate change based on ideas of equity and justice (see chapters six and seven for more on this). For this reason, the forecasts differ quite widely. However, all models and assumptions result in higher temperatures, in some cases by as much as 10.4°F (5.8°C). Given just how much carbon dioxide we've already produced, further warming is inevitable. It is also certain that the temperature increases we can expect in the coming years will outstrip anything we've experienced so far. This means that, whatever global warming has done to your local weather so far, it's going to get a whole lot worse in the years to come. The Earth won't have seen anything this dramatic in at least 10,000 years—possibly a lot longer. To make it even more unpleasant, land areas will warm more than oceans. So, while the news might be less frightening if you're a fish (or if you own an oceangoing boat), for the vast majority of us who live on dry land, the prognosis could hardly be worse. Parts of North America and central Asia, in particular, could end up seeing the mercury rise 40 percent faster than the already high average change that has been forecast globally. And those living in cities will suffer even more due to the "urban heat island" effect (see chapter four).

Whatever You Do, Don't Pray for Rain

Well, not if you're living in the northern United States, Canada, Japan, parts of China or most of Europe, anyway. Much of these heavily populated areas will experience higher levels of precipitation. Chances are, if you're planning something in the great outdoors, it probably *will* rain on your parade—especially if you're doing it in winter, when rainfall is likely to increase more (summers may actually be drier).

However, the impacts of climate change will be far from consistent, particularly when it comes to rainfall. Different regions could experience very different changes in their local weather as the Earth warms up. Those living closer to the equator may have to wait and see what's in store—while some regions may get more rainfall overall, others could well get less. Ironically, in many cases, these are areas that already suffer from a lack of rain. Much of Australia could get less rainfall, particularly in winter, while the Mediterranean could get less over summer, but more in winter. Many tropical areas could get more rain, while the sub-Tropics could actually get less.

Storms Are Brewing in the Skies

Recent years have already seen a rise in extreme weather events. According to the experts, this is just the start. More intense downpours and storms are set to affect many regions, including Europe, North America, South Asia, southern Africa, Australia and the South Pacific. There will also be a widespread increase in the number of heat waves as global warming continues to accelerate, with studies showing that the United States, Canada, Europe and Australia will suffer most. An increase in droughts will hit many regions, too.

Meanwhile, tornadoes, tropical cyclones and hurricanes have also increased in number since the mid-1990s. Although climate models still struggle when it comes to predicting relatively rare events such as hurricanes, experts are now convinced that global warming will continue and even speed up the trend toward extreme weather, so a rise in less common phenomena such as these would certainly fit the overall picture. More worrying still, some scientists now predict that hurricanes and other extreme events could become increasingly intense and powerful as time goes by. In late 2004, a major study by experts from the United States examined how the destructive power of hurricanes might alter as a result of climate change. This study was based on the most comprehensive research on hurricane patterns to date, and made use of the supercomputers at the U.S. Commerce Department's Geophysical Fluid Dynamics Laboratory. According to the supercomputers, the force and intensity of hurricanes is set to rise. In the coming decades, the average hurricane could become half a point stronger on the 1–5 scale used to measure hurricane and storm strength—a major increase. The amount of rainfall resulting from hurricanes will rise, too, by an average of 18 percent. Such changes will only increase the devastation wrought by this frightening weather phenomenon.

The monsoon season that affects large parts of Asia every summer could also change. Although it is probably too early to say for certain what will happen, early studies suggest it will become less predictable, starting and finishing at different times. It could also become increasingly subject to year-on-year variability, becoming more intense in some years, less in others.

Even more extreme changes are possible. For instance, the North Atlantic current that warms much of Europe and America's eastern seaboard could be affected, with potentially deadly consequences (see "What's the Worst That Could Happen?" later in this chapter).

While heat waves, droughts, thunderstorms, flash floods, twisters, hurricanes and other natural disasters are on the rise, it is possible that severe cold snaps and bitter winter storms could happen less often. Unfortunately, even this one ray of hope pales into insignificance when one considers that winter rainstorms and flooding will become more frequent.

Looking still further ahead, the longevity of greenhouse gases in our atmosphere means the world will probably keep getting hotter for many centuries to come. Sea levels could rise by as much as 24 feet (7 meters) in the longer term—something to keep in mind if you're tempted by an apartment on the first two or three floors.

REGION-BY-REGION: YOUR LOCAL WEATHER FORECAST

"A riddle wrapped in a mystery inside an enigma," said Winston Churchill in 1939. He was describing Russia, but he might just as well have been trying to decipher what we can expect to happen to our local weather. While climate experts are increasingly certain about changes at the global or continental level, it remains a lot more difficult to predict what to expect within countries, either regionally or locally. In spite of this, a number of models have been developed in recent years that are finally helping us figure out what we can expect. And of course, we now have data going back at least 150 years telling us what's *already* happened, which can assist in identifying the trends and peculiarities of each region.

How the West Was Wet . . .

With diverse landscapes ranging from beaches to deserts and even mountains, the American west has always had an element of the unpredictable when it comes to the weather. During the past century, temperatures have already started to rise, by up to 5°F in some places. Precipitation has already increased, too, by up to 50 percent in some cases, although this is far from uniform, with parts of Arizona, for instance, on the receiving end of more frequent and severe droughts. Across the entire region, the frequency of heavy downpours has been on the rise since the 1950s. Meanwhile, the amount of snow dumped on high-altitude parts of California and Nevada has slumped, much to the consternation of avid skiers and snowboarders.

Models used to predict the future of the west's weather estimate that average temperatures will jump by 4°F or even more in the next 30 years, and will continue climbing after that. Winters should become a lot wetter, especially over California, while the Rocky Mountains are set to suffer more dry spells. Expect an increase in cloud cover, too, and a jump in the number of extreme bouts of heavy rainfall alternating with extended droughts, sparking an increase in forest fires. Heat waves will go up during the summer months. Sea levels seem certain to rise significantly, too, by as much as three feet (one meter). And, if it continues, the recent spike in El Niño weather patterns will add to the warmer, wetter weather, and to an increase in heavy rain events and flash floods.

. . . and the Pacific Northwest Was Wetter

The Pacific Northwest's reputation for offering a high quality of life and easy access to the great outdoors is undeniable. Even its equally renowned wet weather has failed to put a dampener on its appeal, as the region's rapid population growth clearly demonstrates (it has doubled in 30 years). Actually, the region's rainy reputation is a little unfair, as many places get less than 20 inches (0.5 meters) each year. Sadly, though, this may not last. The Pacific Northwest's precipitation problem has only intensified in recent times. Annual precipitation has gone up by 10 percent across the region as a whole in recent decades, and as much as 40 percent in eastern Washington and parts of Idaho. Average temperatures have also increased, by 3°F in some places. And in spite of giant leaps forward in our understanding of meteorology, the weather has become less easy to predict, too, with greater annual fluctuations experienced. Many scientists point to the recent influence of El Niño and La Niña as part of the cause.

Looking ahead, most projections for the region suggest that climate change will bring precipitation increases of up to 50 percent over the region as a whole—a dramatic shift. This will be far from universal, though, with some places actually suffering from slight drops in rainfall. Winters will be wetter, while summers could actually end up drier. As with many other places, temperatures are set to go up, a lot. Sea-level rise (and flooding) are likely to be considerable.

Great Plains, Great Problems

Over the past century, temperatures in Montana, North Dakota and South Dakota have climbed by as much as 5.5°F. However, they have changed very little in the southern Great Plains. Rainfall has gone up slightly overall, and Texas in particular has received more heavy downpours. In the coming years, temperatures will rise across the entire region, particularly in the west. Rainfall will increase, especially in the north. Extreme weather events are set to rise, and the region can expect a lot more droughts, heat waves and flooding.

Midwest—"Rain, Rain Go Away"

Would the old nursery rhyme, "rain, rain, go away, come again another day" work in the Midwest? Fat chance. Precipitation already jumped by as much as one fifth last century, with eastern parts of the region particularly affected. In spite of some local variations, it is possible it will increase again by as much as one third in the coming decades.

Surprisingly, though, the last 100 years actually saw some parts of the Midwest, particularly around the Ohio River Valley, become marginally colder. No such luck for the northern Midwest, however—it warmed up quite a bit, and will continue to do so. Heavy storms, flash floods and heat waves will intensify and become more frequent in the coming years, although winter temperatures may become less extreme.

Is the Northeast Going to Extremes?

The Northeast has always been a place of extremes, from the urban jungles of Manhattan to the leafy tranquility of Vermont. Weatherwise, it's been a similar story. For a start, recent years have seen great variability in the weather, with a discernible increase in storms, floods, droughts and heat waves. Overall, temperature changes have been patchy, and although rainfall has increased, the amount of winter snowfall has dropped.

As for the future, experts seem uncertain about how the mercury could be affected, but most are predicting a relatively low rate of warming compared to many other regions. In spite of year-on-year variability, and one or two unpleasant seasons lately, winters may become more mild over the long term, with fewer cold snaps (although some models predict an increase in the frequency and intensity of winter storms). Most models predict a rise in extreme weather, such as storms and heat waves, which is obviously a major concern. Just to make life even more exciting, there is likely to be more rain, especially in winter. Sea levels will rise significantly, bringing coastal flooding and erosion. It's hard to find a positive side to all of this, but at least the weather seems to confirm the old truism that "everything happens in New York." And with all the climatic changes going on, perhaps inhabitants of the Big Apple and their neighbors in Boston, Buffalo and elsewhere will soon be able to match the British when it comes to talking about the changing weather.

For the Southeast, "Twister" Isn't a Game

The mercury has been rising rapidly in the Southeast for the past 30 years, with higher precipitation recorded in many areas going back even further, particularly in the Gulf states. El Niño and La Niña weather patterns have also intruded increasingly into the region, creating an unpredictable concoction of warmer, wetter weather one year, followed by colder conditions the next. In recent years, the number of twisters has risen dramatically.

Experts are uncertain on what the future might bring, but some scenarios point to huge increases in temperatures over the next few decades. With El Niño and La Niña still not fully understood (see the next section), their impact remains uncertain. More rainfall will hit some regions, while dry periods and droughts will affect others, particularly in the South. More heat waves can be expected, too, along with floods and possibly even hurricanes. Those areas affected by twisters would do well to step up their preparations to deal with this problem; while it is too soon to take it as a long-term trend, a big jump in the number of tornadoes in recent years should be sounding alarms in some quarters. Sea-level rise is certain, and could well happen rapidly.

EL NIÑO AND CLIMATE CHANGE

El Niño. You've probably heard your local television weather presenter refer to it time and again, usually just before they tell you bad weather's on the way. But if you're still not exactly sure what it is, don't worry—you're definitely not alone. Even the experts are still far from certain about some aspects of this unusual weather phenomenon.

What the experts *can* tell you is that El Niño is a complex weather event in the Pacific Ocean that affects the weather across the entire globe, impacting almost everywhere from the United States to Australia, New Zealand and even Africa and the Atlantic Ocean. El Niño weakens the usual trade winds that blow westward across the Pacific Ocean. This has a series of complex flow-on effects that can eventually lead to temperatures rising by as much as 9°F above average and to overall increases in rainfall. The term "El Niño," which is Spanish for "Little Boy" but can also mean "Baby Jesus," was originally coined by Peruvian fishermen because the phenomenon tends to begin around Christmas. The weather cycles involved are far from regular, though, and can change both in terms of strength and timing. There are great variations in how El Niño affects different countries and regions, too, with flooding often resulting in Peru, more storms in the southern United States from California all the way to Florida, and droughts in Australia and Indonesia.

El Niño is not something new. Indeed, it is a natural part of the region's climate system. What has changed, though, is how frequently the phenomenon has been occurring. Since the 1970s, it has become far more common and intense. While there are several theories about why this should be the case, a growing number of experts now believe that it is connected to climate change. An earlier theory that it was caused by volcanic eruptions, such as that of Mount Pinatubo in the Philippines in June 1991, has since been rejected.

A second weather phenomenon known as La Niña (the Little Girl) often follows El Niño. Unlike El Niño, La Niña often results in colder weather, with average temperatures dropping by an average 7°F.

Recent El Niño weather patterns were detected in 1986–1987, 1991–1992, 1997–1998, and 2002–2003. Unfortunately, in spite of receiving a lot of attention from climatologists in recent years, El Niño and La Niña are still not fully understood. Their links to climate change are not clear, either. While we know that El Niño and La Niña are not caused by climate change, most climatologists agree that global warming is likely to change the way these two weather phenomena behave. Given the interconnections within the world's climate system, it would be strange if it didn't. Some experts now believe the El Niño–La Niña phenomenon will strengthen and become more intense over time, possibly making already wet areas (mostly in North and South America) prone to further precipitation, while dry areas (particularly in parts of Asia and Australia) will become still more vulnerable to drought. The timing of these weather patterns could become even more unpredictable.

WHAT'S THE WORST THAT COULD HAPPEN?

The likely changes to our weather described above have been widely endorsed by most climate experts. The predictions are based on models approved by the Intergovernmental Panel on Climate Change and other respected groups of experts. But, bad though they may seem, these are not the worst we may have to face. In recent years, theories of "abrupt" climate change have begun to circulate. While these have not yet become mainstream science, most credible experts are unwilling to dismiss them, and some now see them as a distinct possibility.

These theories argue that the Earth is reaching a crisis point where it will simply be unable to cope with what we're throwing at its atmosphere. If we push the planet to its breaking point, the theory goes, then the climate could change dramatically, and in a very short space of time—far more quickly even than the changes predicted in more mainstream forecasts.

Old-time crooner Bing Crosby was probably right when he said we should always "accentuate the positive" and "eliminate the negative." After all, why dwell on the worst scenario if it might never happen? It's a good point. On the other hand, though, Crosby had never heard of global warming, and in this case, it might pay to know what the most unpleasant scenarios could involve, especially as they're starting to be taken more seriously by the experts. So, what's the worst that could happen?

Why Global Warming Could Leave You Cold

For a start, some places could actually get colder—a lot colder. One of the reasons why the experts prefer to refer to the phenomenon as "climate change" rather than "global warming" is that, while most places are starting to heat up, this won't happen everywhere. In some of the more extreme scenarios, climate change could result in a big freeze for many of us, even causing a new Ice Age. The thinking behind this prediction is that climate change has the potential to slow down or even stop a benign weather phenomenon in the Atlantic Ocean known as the "Gulf Stream." This is a vast current of warmer air and weather that flows into the North Atlantic from the Tropics. It keeps the eastern United States and western Europe far warmer than they might otherwise be. Without it, places like New England and the UK could suddenly get a whole lot colder.

Now, some experts think there's a chance this change might actually happen. The reason for this is that the North Atlantic current relies on a complex series of factors that "pull" the warmer water and weather north. As the warmer current heads north, it gradually loses its heat into the atmosphere, cooling and becoming denser the further it travels. The current then sinks down into the ocean, pulling further water from the Tropics to fill the gap in a sort of "conveyor belt" process.

The problem now, though, is that global warming is causing glaciers to melt in the Arctic. This is releasing freshwater into the North Atlantic, which is reducing the level of salinity in the ocean. This is a concern because the Atlantic "conveyor belt" system that carries warm air north is believed to be very sensitive to salt levels, which affect the water's density. The melting glaciers and an increase in rainfall could affect salinity levels to such a degree that the density of the water changes, stopping the cooling water from sinking into the ocean depths as it heads north. This in turn would reduce the "pull" of the North Atlantic current.

If the theory is right, the complex changes to rainfall and salt levels in the North Atlantic could stop warmer weather coming north. More worrying still, it's happened before, although not for at least 8,000 years. Back then, a mini–Ice Age occurred, throwing our early ancestors a curveball in the shape of significantly colder weather—as much as 20°F colder, which is a huge drop. Time to dig out that old hot water bottle and furry hat, perhaps?

California Burning, Parched in El Paso

Elsewhere, the picture might be different, but no less bleak, if rapid climate change happened. Imagine droughts afflicting much of the world, including the southern and western United States. The result would be water and food shortages on a scale we've never faced before—at least, not if we've been living in wealthy parts of the world like the United States, Canada or Europe. Now try increasing the number of forest fires by, say, ten times because of the drier weather. Tens of thousands of homes, even hundreds of thousands, would be faced with the threat of fires every year; emergency services would be stretched to the breaking point; hospitals would be filled with those affected. Suddenly, California might not be such an attractive place to live.

The nightmare scenario of abrupt climate change was the subject of a recent report commissioned by veteran Defense Department insider Andrew Marshall and written by Doug Randall and Peter Schwartz, consultants who have worked for big business and (in Schwartz's case) the CIA.

"We Begin Bombing in Five Minutes"

The report considers a worst-case scenario about what the future might look like in 2020 if abrupt climate change happens in the next few years. As their report was for the Pentagon, Randall and Schwartz focused on the security and defense implications such a change might have, conjuring up visions of famines, water shortages and other disasters that could lead to the global breakdown of law and order, full-scale wars and even nuclear conflict. Their dire warnings were based on changes to our weather that include sudden temperature drops of up to 5°F in parts of North America and Asia and 6°F in Europe. The report suggests a dramatic rise in extreme weather events, particularly storms, that ravage coastal areas of western Europe and the United States. In their worst-case scenario, low-lying areas in places such as Holland and Britain, the eastern seaboard and California in North America, are overrun by regular flooding. Many major cities, from Los Angeles to Amsterdam, are affected; some become virtually uninhabitable due to flooding and sea-level rise.

Meanwhile, so-called megadroughts strike much of the world, including the south and west of the United States. Wind speeds increase, causing dust storms and the loss of fertile topsoil needed to make crops grow. While the United States and Europe have the wealth and resources to cope better than some other places, both suffer from economic pressures and wave after wave of immigrants from other parts of the world that are suffering even more. The consequences for the United States and European economies are significant, and social unrest increases as countries begin to slip into recession, unemployment rises and wage and salary growth becomes a thing of the past.

Other parts of the world, including Africa, Latin America and Asia, are hurt still more—but their suffering soon makes itself felt in the United States and Europe, as oil supplies and world trade become threatened by global instability. The world soon splits into regional blocs or, worse, anarchy. Nowhere is left unaffected. Tens of millions die. The world is irrevocably changed. And, rather than it happening in our children or grandchildren's time, as many experts fear, it actually happens to us.

So What Are the Chances?

But just how likely are these kinds of doomsday scenarios? Will abrupt climate change strike soon? Is disaster closer than most of the experts imagine?

Probably not. Climate change is happening, and happening fast; the impacts will increase as each year passes, and we certainly need to act now. But, the major changes described above are far more likely to happen over decades, rather than weeks or months.

Still, it could happen. Even the Intergovernmental Panel on Climate Change, which represents mainstream scientific opinion, refuses to rule out such a scenario.

"The possibility for rapid and irreversible changes in the climate system exists, but there is a large degree of uncertainty about the mechanisms involved and hence also about the likelihood or time-scales of such transitions," it concluded in 2001. In spite of the obvious uncertainties, therefore, the Panel was clearly concerned about the risks of pushing the planet over the edge in terms of climate change. "There is evidence from polar ice cores suggesting that atmospheric regimes can change within a few years and that large-scale hemispheric changes can evolve as fast as a few decades," it warned, pointing out, too, that major changes have happened before. For instance, the Sahara, which had previously been a very fertile area, suddenly turned to desert in a very short space of time about 5,500 years ago due to changes to the climate.

WEATHERING THE STORM

It is clear that things are starting to heat up for most of us, and that the number of droughts, storms, floods, heat waves and other extreme events is on the rise, too. But it doesn't stop there. As the next chapter explains, the continuing changes to our weather are having a frightening impact on everything around us.

CHAPTER THREE

WHAT IS GLOBAL WARMING DOING TO MY WORLD?

"Over a million species could be threatened with extinction as a result of climate change."

—Professor Chris Thomas, lead author of the report *Extinction Risk from Climate Change,* 2004

There is no longer any doubt about climate change. The evidence is clear, the science is certain. Rising average temperatures and an increase in the number of extreme weather events such as killer heat waves, intense rain storms and flooding is already becoming more common. These trends are set to continue, and even accelerate, as the years pass.

But could changes to our weather really threaten the existence of over a million species, as Professor Thomas claims? It's hard to imagine. According to Professor Thomas and his fellow experts, this means up to 37 percent of animal and plant species in six regions around the world will be wiped out by 2050 because they will be unable to adapt to the rapid changes we are causing to the planet's climate. So how is it possible that such a huge proportion of the world's plants and animals could be extinguished in our lifetime just because of a few changes to our weather?

To start with, the changes happening in our atmosphere are anything but small. In a short space of time, our use of fossil fuels has had a significant effect on the global climate. Since 1998 we have registered the four hottest years in at least the last century-and-a-half, and possibly for the past two millennia. Average temperatures have climbed 1.1°F (0.6°C) in the last century, much of it since the mid-1970s. Extreme weather events have started to increase in number and strength, as any Californian affected by the storms and flooding that struck in early 2005 will testify. What's more, while our planet is far from fragile, it is sensitive to change—and changes to the global climate are a big deal. Such changes have flow-on effects that can totally disrupt entire habitats and ecosystems, as well as the plants and animals (including humans) that live in them. Already, climate change has started to affect the wider world in some worrying ways, from melting in the Arctic to the death of coral reefs to changes in growing seasons and animal habitats and migration patterns everywhere from New England to New Zealand. From butterflies to polar bears to beech trees, almost every form of life appears to be vulnerable to its influence.

ARCTIC ANXIETY

In late 2003, scientists from the United States and Canada announced that the largest ice shelf in the Arctic had broken up. The Ward Hunt Ice Shelf to the north of Canada's Ellesmere Island had split into two main parts, with other large blocks of ice also pulling away from the main sections. This was not the first time scientists had reported evidence that global warming was having a major impact on the polar icecaps. Actually, it was just the tip of the iceberg. Warmer weather throughout the year was melting the Arctic's massive ice sheets at a rapid rate. According to the Intergovernmental Panel on Climate Change, the sea ice around the North Pole has now thinned out by as much as 40 percent in recent decades. It continues to do so, losing as much as one-tenth of its permanent ice cover every ten years. By the end of the century, there could easily be no permanent ice left in the Arctic at all. In Alaska alone, 500 cubic miles of ice have disappeared since the 1950s.

Further evidence of this remarkable change was revealed in October 2004 with the release of satellite information exposing more "extreme" ice loss, especially in northern Alaska and eastern Siberia. According to researchers from the University of Colorado, this new satellite data showed the area covered by floating sea ice in the Arctic receding more than 13 percent—the third straight year to register extreme ice losses.

"The Earth is literally melting," announced Sheila Watt-Cloutier, a native Inuit leader representing communities living near the Arctic, in an address to the U.S. Senate's Commerce Committee in September 2004. Watt-Cloutier told senators of major changes in climate and to flora and fauna in the Arctic and predicted that this was a sign of things to come for the rest of the world.

She is right. So far, some of the greatest warming has happened in areas close to the Arctic—far higher than the average global change of 1.1°F. That's because these areas previously had a lot of snow or ice, which reflects sunlight back into the atmosphere. Because some of this reflective surface has been lost, more heat is being absorbed in that part of the world—a trend that is predicted to continue for a long time to come and could lead the region to heat up 40 percent more rapidly than most other places. Scientists believe that in the distant past natural periods of warming have melted the poles and brought on rapid temperature increases of as much as 20°F. Unfortunately, Watt-Cloutier's warning apparently fell on deaf ears, and U.S. politicians were subsequently accused not only of ignoring the warnings, but of actually blocking a report recommending urgent action to deal with climate change in the Arctic. This is a tragedy, because Watt-Cloutier was absolutely right about the impact climate change is having on local flora and fauna. The entire food chain has been disrupted. Polar bears, seals, whales, walruses and countless species of fish and other ocean life have been affected—as have the communities of people that depend on fishing for their survival.

There are also fears of the impact it is having on plankton, the oceanic micro-organisms that are the basis of the whole marine food chain. A study of the North Sea by British experts in 2004 found that cod and some other fish species, as well as sea birds such as kittiwakes and guillemots, were failing fast, with no obvious explanation. Scientists were unable to account for these deaths, but suspected the reason had something to do with climate change. They theorized that global warming was having an impact on plankton populations and their distribution. Apparently, the cold-water plankton that the fish in this area feed on are shifting northward or dying off. This is altering the entire food chain for every creature in the North Sea, from fish to whales to sea birds. People are being seriously impacted by such changes, too. The transformation of the world's ecosystems and plant and animal life due to climate change is having major flow-on effects in terms of our economic development and even our health (see chapter four for more on this). In this particular case, a major food supply and source of economic livelihood is under threat, risking jobs in many coastal towns and villages that rely on the fishing industry as a source of income.

Other habitats in the far north have changed irrevocably, too. For instance, a bug that was once rarely found in the far north, the spruce bark beetle, has spread due to the warmer weather, and is now devastating millions of acres of Alaskan forests—its preferred meal. Meanwhile, a major study by the International Institute for Sustainable Development in northern Canada found that the big freeze that usually hits the area in the fall now happens a month later than it used to due to warmer weather, while the spring thaw is felt a lot earlier. As a result, the sea ice is further away from the community of native Inuvialuit hunters and trappers who live there, taking with it the seals they rely on for food. Warmer summers are melting the Arctic permafrost and causing inland lakes to bleed freshwater into the ocean, killing the freshwater fish population. Barn swallows, robins and other species of birds are migrating to the region, while new fish species are arriving. Flies and mosquitoes are also thriving there for the first time, too, bringing new diseases in their wake. Everything is being thrown out of kilter.

Such changes haven't been confined to the Arctic and neighboring areas. Half a world away in the Southern Hemisphere, Antarctica's Pine Island Glacier—one of the world's biggest—was found to be slipping into the sea far faster than had earlier been predicted. Such glaciers are not small—some are the size of countries. In 2002, a huge chunk of the Larsen B Ice Shelf, larger than Rhode Island, sheered off into the ocean and broke up in less than a month—a speed that shocked many experts. Glaciologist David Vaughan observed at the time that the speed at which the melting took place was "staggering," with 500 million tons of ice sheet disintegrating in just a few weeks. Some fear the eventual collapse of the West Antarctic ice sheet, too, which would lead to catastrophic changes in sea levels. Fortunately, though, mainstream scientists consider this apocalyptic scenario unlikely, at least for the foreseeable future.

Glaciers in other parts of the world *have* been melting rapidly, though. Around the world, the regions that can boast snow cover have seen it recede by an average of 10 percent in the last 40 years. Montana's glaciers are quickly melting away and could disappear entirely in the coming decades. So are those in Central Asia, where glaciers are losing more than one cubic mile of ice every year. The same is true in places as far flung as Nepal, Switzerland, Bolivia and Patagonia. Venezuela had 6 glaciers 30 years ago. Now, it has only 2. Africa's famous Mount Kilimanjaro has lost three-quarters of its ice cap in the last century, and could well say goodbye to the rest by 2015. Meanwhile, the glaciers in the European Alps have shrunk by 50 percent since the start of the Industrial Revolution. Again, such changes can have all sorts of flow-on effects, from displacing plant and animal species, to threatening local communities with flooding, to a loss of freshwater that could jeopardize future supplies of this precious commodity.

THAT SINKING FEELING

The effects of glacial and ice sheet melting are not only being felt locally. The disintegration of the glaciers and snow cover is also having a profound effect globally. The most obvious change is to our oceans and coasts. The Ward Hunt Ice Shelf alone released huge amounts of freshwater when it began to break up and melt, draining water into the ocean that had previously been locked up inland. It has contributed to the release of thousands of square miles of ice melting into our seas. What's more, the oceans are warming, too, as a result of climate change. This is bad news because when ocean water warms up, it expands. Combined with the glacial melting, it has caused seas to rise around our coastlines by 8 inches (20 centimeters) on average.

This might not sound like much, but just a small change can affect coastal areas, sometimes with horrific consequences. In Shishmaref, a small Alaskan village near the Arctic Circle, the tide has already encroached a further 100 yards inland in recent years, damaging many houses. Now, the entire community is considering shifting the village inland. Thousands of miles away, the tropical Maldives—a popular tourist resort in the Indian Ocean—is also threatened by sea-level rise that is making some of the country's many islands uninhabitable. Most of the Maldives is less than three feet above sea level. The Pacific Island nation of Tuvalu is suffering from serious flooding, too; most of it is barely above sea level, meaning a lot of it could eventually end up totally submerged. The problem is so serious that its larger neighbor, New Zealand, has offered to allow the entire population of 11,000 people to emigrate there, should their own nation sink beneath the waves. Some believe this will happen within a generation.

Other parts of the world are being affected, too. In North America, sea-level rise and an increasing number of storms and extreme weather is affecting many coastal areas, from California to Florida to New England. In North Carolina, a lighthouse built 130 years ago 300 yards inland—the distance of three football fields placed end-to-end—had to be moved when it was realized the ocean had advanced to within just 50 yards. The same process is happening in parts of western Europe, including the Netherlands and southern England, as well as large stretches of coastline in Africa and Asia. Bangladesh, for instance, is already experiencing the encroachment of the ocean as it eats into the country's coasts. It could lose 17 percent of its entire territory to the ocean's advance in the coming years. Around the world, 70 percent of all sandy coastlines have been in retreat as the waters rise.

And that is just the start: by the end of the century, a further rise of as much as 37 inches, or 3 feet, is predicted as snow and ice loss continues and the seas become warmer still. The U.S. Environmental Protection Agency estimates that such a change would flood more than 20,000 square miles of American territory. While the effects will be most strongly felt in places such as Florida, Texas, Louisiana and North Carolina, almost all areas close to the shoreline and to rivers will be at risk. One study suggests that seawater will encroach 400 feet inland in low-lying parts of Florida. Britain's chief scientific adviser, Sir David King, has warned that sea-level rise could eventually drown the sites of major cities such as London, New York and New Orleans. Warning that greenhouse gas concentrations are at their highest in 55 million years—when there was no ice on the planet at all—he predicted that London and New York could be among the "first to go."

If the polar regions did melt, and bear in mind that sea-level rise is expected to continue for hundreds of years in most scenarios, then we could expect to see seas rise by as much as 23 feet (7 meters). While we won't be around to see it, it is hardly the best inheritance to leave our great-great-grandchildren—unless we buy a house halfway up a mountain, of course.

SEA LIFE . . . SEE DEATH

So our coastal areas are already altering, and could change dramatically as the sea encroaches ever further inland across the globe. But what about the rest of our world? One of the most difficult parts of the planet to study are our oceans. Making up more than 70 percent of the world's surface, and sinking into inky-black recesses many miles deep, much of it remains unexplored and unknown. It has complex ecosystems and food chains that even the experts have only partially figured out and life forms we do not even know about.

What we do know, though, is that the increase in carbon dioxide emissions over the past two centuries is causing some changes that could have a major impact, not only in the ocean's depths, but on the rest of the planet, too. According to research published in 2004 by the U.S. National Oceanic and Atmospheric Administration, a hidden transformation in the chemistry of our oceans is occurring as a consequence of climate change. Scientists have discovered that almost *half* the carbon dioxide entering our atmosphere is being absorbed by the oceans. While this has helped slow global warming on the Earth's surface, it has also caused major changes in the chemistry of the sea, threatening marine life. Corals, mollusks and some types of plankton appear to have been particularly affected so far. But as such species form the basis of the ocean's food chain, it is certain that the effects will flow through to the rest of the plant and animal kingdom, too. Already, there are signs that many other species are being affected. A study published by the United Nations Environment Program in early 2004 suggested that the world's oceans now have areas so profoundly affected by human activities that they've become "dead zones." Experts identified 150 of these zones in areas as diverse as the Gulf of Mexico, Chesapeake Bay, the Baltic Sea and the Gulf of Thailand. According to the UN, these zones lack the necessary oxygen that many fish, oysters and other marine creatures need to survive. The UN blamed the loss of oxygen in these areas on an excess of nitrogen, which had been caused by our burgeoning use of agricultural fertilizers, waste products entering the ocean and—you guessed it—vehicle and factory emissions, which are also the major cause of climate change.

Just months earlier, the U.S. Congress received a report from the independent Pew Oceans Commission warning of a "silent collapse" in the health of ocean and coastal habitats, with problems being observed across the entire food chain. The Commission, which was chaired by former White House Chief of Staff Leon Panetta, and whose members included New York Governor George Pataki and several prominent environmentalists, blamed climate change, too much commercial fishing, pollution and a general misuse of the environment by humankind.

"The ability of our oceans to support life as it does now may be in the process of being permanently altered," warned Amy Mathews-Amos and Ewann Berntson of Seattle's Marine Conservation Biology Institute in a recent report. "Global warming could be the knock-out punch for many species which are already under stress from over-fishing and habitat loss," they added. This would impact on humans, too, as our oceans are an abundant source of food and medicines, as well as a source of income through tourism and fishing. Worst hit so far are species at higher latitudes, where the warming has been the most obvious. For instance, salmon populations in the North Pacific have already fallen away markedly.

REEF MADNESS

One habitat where the impact of climate change is easy to measure is our coral reefs. These reefs, which can be found in places as far-flung as the coasts of Australia and the Caribbean, are among the world's most stunning natural wonders. Providing a home to countless species of fish and plant life—a quarter of all marine life according to some estimates—they are loved by scuba divers for their natural beauty. Coral reefs develop in a unique way, when tiny animals called polyps, which live in shallow water, die off and form rock-like corals. Over time, enough of these little creatures die that their skeletons form the basis of entire reefs, which then provide habitats for a multitude of flora and fauna. But this takes time, and coral reefs are one of the oldest types of habitat for life on Earth, growing over many thousands of years. Australia's Great Barrier Reef, for instance, was formed over five million years.

Amazingly, though, we've managed to destroy one-quarter of them in just a few decades. As for the rest, well, experts believe most of these are now under threat, too. According to one Australian study, less than 5 percent of the Great Barrier Reef will be left by 2050 if we fail to deal with the problem. Climate change isn't the only concern, with over-fishing and many other human activities also contributing to the problem. But global warming is a particular thorn in the side, as rising temperatures kill the microscopic algae that are crucial to any reef's survival. The result is that reefs turn white and die in a process known as coral bleaching.

"Coral reefs are one of the first major casualties of climate change," observed Professor Ove Hoegh-Guldberg of the University of Queensland, Australia, who coauthored a report on the threat to the Great Barrier Reef.

THE LAND YOU CALL HOME?

Closer to home, many changes are being observed on land, too. Eventually, they might alter things so much you won't even recognize the place. On the surface, though, what's happened so far seems harmless enough. So what if spring starts a little sooner, and fall arrives late? Isn't it nice to see flowers budding earlier in the year, or to have a few less freezing winter days? After all, humans can adapt to change—surely animals and plants will, too?

It is certainly true that some species will adapt; some will even thrive. For instance, certain bugs will spread further north and south, including a few rather eye-catching butterflies. Sounds nice, no? Unfortunately, they won't be the only ones, as they are joined by insects like mosquitoes that can carry diseases such as malaria and West Nile Virus. Where certain life forms exist will change, too. For instance, beech trees may dwindle in some parts of North America and Europe due to warmer weather, to be replaced by trees and plants suited to the higher temperatures. But what of the birds and insects that feed off the beech? If the trees they need disappear, what will become of the animals that depend on them? And what of the changes in breeding seasons for animals or growing seasons for plants? What impact will they have on other parts of the food chain?

In many cases, we really don't know, for sure. Judging by what we've seen so far, though, the news is not good. Entire habitats will change, are already changing, plants and animals will be under pressure to adapt rapidly to a transformation that comes not from nature, but from us. Many will not be able to change in time. According to the conservation group WWF, climate change has already claimed its first victim; the Costa Rican golden toad is now extinct.

It is only the beginning. Many natural habitats are already under stress, and the animals that inhabit them are coming under pressure, too. The Intergovernmental Panel on Climate Change predicts that many types of habitat could undergo "significant and irreversible damage." Vulnerable ecosystems include our forests, wetlands, grassland areas and prairies.

Run Forest, Run!

It's a shame they can't run away, because frankly, forests are in serous trouble. Trees are very sensitive to climatic conditions. And unlike the animals that live in them, it's a lot more difficult for trees to scurry to safety. Tests show that a modest temperature change of just 2°F affects the way forests function, and which species will thrive, or die. Some trees, such as fir and maple trees, do well in cooler climates; as the planet warms, they are feeling the pinch in some places, but starting to prosper in new areas further north. This is having flow-on effects not just for the trees, but for the entire community of plants and animals that inhabit these areas.

Nor is it just warmer temperatures that are having an impact. Changing rainfall patterns are making a difference, too. Other risks include the spread of new threats to forests, including different bugs and diseases that are drifting into new areas. Meanwhile, in places that are set to experience drier summers, such as parts of California and the Rocky Mountains, forest fires are rising in number, and will continue to do so, posing a major threat to many forest ecosystems.

Another part of the forestry equation is the role trees play in combating climate change. Plants pull in and store carbon dioxide from the air around them and also produce oxygen in a process known as photosynthesis—their version of eating and breathing. As carbon dioxide is the main cause of climate change, the fact that trees and other plants capture this gas and pull it out of the atmosphere is helping offset some of the damage we've been doing in spewing more and more of the stuff from our cars, factories and homes. Unfortunately, though, when a forest starts to alter its composition and the types of trees that inhabit it change, large amounts of carbon are lost into the atmosphere—which only makes the problem worse.

One positive message the experts had taken from all of this in the past was that a world with more carbon dioxide in the atmosphere would actually make it easier for forests and plants to grow. As plants love carbon as much as we humans love oxygen, it would certainly make a lot of sense. More atmospheric carbon is believed to help trees and plants mature more quickly, which, in turn, could potentially mean that trees absorb extra carbon dioxide, therefore helping out even more in the struggle to contain climate change. The bad news, though, is that researchers recently discovered that the net impact would not be as positive as they had imagined. Their studies of the Amazon confirmed that changes in atmospheric carbon dioxide levels are causing the forests to change. But while new trees are growing more quickly, existing trees are dying faster. What's worse, the researchers found that fast-growing trees generally capture less carbon than slow-growing ones, meaning forests' carbon storing capacity could actually be reduced. This means forests could well become less useful in combating climate change than had previously been thought, despite the greater number of fast-growing trees.

While the impact of climate change on our forests is worrying enough, it is not the only problem forests face. Humans have been cutting down trees in vast numbers for centuries. In spite of recent efforts to protect our trees, we are still stripping our forests away in many parts of the world at an alarming rate, chopping down 16 million hectares in the Amazon and other parts of the world every year. Climate change is simply making a bad problem worse. It is hardly a surprise, then, that the prognosis for our forests is not good. With a human population that's grown from 2.5 billion to 6.5 billion in less than 50 years, the temptation to exploit our forests is just too great—for many people, it is simply a case of survival. The consequences of all this exploitation and over-use are not hard to find; in just one part of Brazil, a staggering 2,000 different species of native trees are now threatened with extinction.

Sea-level rise will also have an impact on forests near our coasts. On the Gulf of Mexico's shoreline, for instance, the incursion of the oceans has brought saltwater to the nearby forests, killing trees across parts of southern Florida and Louisiana. Meanwhile, the growing number of fierce storms, floods and other extreme weather events can be expected to have an impact on forests in every part of the world.

Bogged Down

Wetlands, bogs, fens, swamps and marshes are being seriously affected by climate change, too, particularly as a result of sea-level rise and the growing frequency and intensity of storms, floods and other extreme weather events. If you're not full of sympathy for the troubles of the bayou or the quandary of the quagmire, though, you're not alone. These places are not exactly glamorous, and have always had a bad reputation as disagreeable places most people in their right minds wouldn't go anywhere near. Let's face it, they hardly make ideal vacation destinations and, frankly, some of them smell. Popular culture has them down as the hideouts of villains and miscreants. These repulsive places provided the hound of the Baskervilles with its lair and the sinister Magwitch with a place of refuge in the Dickens classic *Great Expectations*. Meanwhile, poor Frodo Baggins almost drowned in one in *The Lord of the Rings— The Two Towers*. Nasty places for hobbits or any other form of life, you might think.

Actually, no; wetlands provide a home for countless animal and plant species, and are recognized for their major contribution to the planet's biological diversity, not to mention their contribution to the global economy. They provide freshwater, food and incomes for millions of people around the world. Their importance was recognized before climate change was even suspected, and an international treaty known as the Ramsar Convention on Wetlands—named after the town of Ramsar, in Iran, where it was signed—was set up to protect them back in the early 1970s. Today, 144 countries have joined the pact, including the United States, Britain, Germany, Japan and China. All have pledged to protect key wetlands areas, and 122 million hectares of land around the world are designated as special conservation zones.

Climate change is a significant threat to these ecosystems, though, especially in coastal zones. Some wetlands are being harmed in areas that are getting less rainfall, too. Again, the loss of these habitats will have major flow-on effects for the plants and animals that inhabit them, and on human populations.

Dry As a Bone

Another quite different type of habitat that is being influenced by climate change are deserts and arid areas. Far from being damaged, though, these forbidding places will thrive and expand. In many places, climate change will make deserts become hotter and drier. They could also continue to encroach on more fertile land close by that was previously covered in grass or crops, making the land un-inhabitable for many species, including humans. This process, known as desertification, is not just a result of climate change, but what we are doing to the weather is certainly helping the process along. As the deserts expand in places like the Sahara and the Asian Steppes, animals, plants and people will be forced out in search of a less hostile environment.

ANIMALS ATTACKED

It should be clear by now that climate change is altering our world. Plant life and trees are changing, seasons are shifting and entire habitats are being transformed, in some cases beyond all recognition. The changes to our forests, grasslands, coasts, oceans, deserts, mountains—to pretty much every part of the planet, in fact—are affecting animal populations all along the food chain. Sadly, though, global warming is not the only problem.

"Climate change is only one of a long list of pressures on wildlife," observed James J. McCarthy and his colleagues from the Intergovernmental Panel on Climate Change in 2001. McCarthy also highlighted other man-made problems such as pollution, the spread of human populations into new parts of the world, urban development, the wholesale destruction of animals' natural habitats and a dramatic increase in fishing and hunting. There is also the illegal trade in endangered wildlife. For instance, the Environmental Investigation Agency warned in October 2004 that the illicit hunting and sale of tigers for their pelts was raging "out of control," mostly due to growing demand from wealthy Chinese. The Agency warned that tiger populations in the wild had plunged from 100,000 a century ago to just 5,000 today. Meanwhile, the relentless felling of our forests, for instance, drives the animals that live in this type of habitat into ever smaller spaces. So far, four-fifths of the world's forest cover has been cleared by people. We have also introduced species into areas where they never existed before, species that often prey on the native birds or animals.

Threats to a multitude of animal species have been reported in every part of the globe. In Australia, 200 types of butterfly are at risk of oblivion, while others could see their numbers and distribution decline markedly. Some amphibians and reptiles are not faring so well, either, including the Boyd's forest dragon, a type of lizard that is high on the list of threatened species as a result of changing temperatures that it cannot cope with. Meanwhile, many birds are suffering due to a change in their traditional habitats and the impact of warmer seasons on their breeding and migration patterns. Certain types of magpies, starlings, finches and warblers are at risk in Europe, while the pygmy owl is threatened in Mexico. The Scottish crossbill may have to leave Scotland permanently if it is to survive, although experts don't seem confident about its future prospects. If it does manage to adapt, it could end up 500 miles away, and we may, in all likelihood, have to change its name to the Icelandic crossbill.

Some of the changes that are taking place are unpredictable if not downright bizarre. For instance, American trout and salmon are set to disappear from many streams and rivers because the cold water in which they thrive is gradually warming up. Estimates by conservation groups Defenders of Wildlife and the Natural Resources Defense Council suggest there could up to 38 percent fewer trout and salmon as their streams become a little warmer, with the greatest losses expected in the South, Southwest and Northeast. To the country's ten million salmon and trout anglers, that could spell disaster—not to mention the costs to the economy of losing a business valued at up to $14 billion a year.

IN THIS TOGETHER?

Calculating the exact cost of what we are doing to our planet's flora and fauna is not easy. For a start, we don't really know how many species are actually out there. Experts believe it could be in the region of 10 million; but so far, we've only identified 1.5 million of them. Some will disappear without us even knowing of their existence. Even so, the impact of their loss on us could turn out to be considerable.

With the world's many habitats and forms of life so interconnected, it is clear that rapid changes to our climate are setting in motion a worrying chain of events. Predictions that over a million species could become extinct should not seem outlandish, given what we are doing to the climate in particular and to our world in general. Of course, extinctions are nothing new; it is the natural order of things that some animals die out, while others evolve and survive. But not like this. It is never natural or normal when you're looking at extinctions on a scale not witnessed in 65 million years—and when just one species is the cause. Experts believe there have been five apocalyptic episodes in the Earth's distant past when mass extinctions have struck. All resulted from some major natural traumatic event, such as a meteorite strike.

Humans weren't around for any of those; but we are causing this one. According to the World Conservation Union, an international environmental group, one in eight birds, one-seventh of all flowering plants, and a quarter of all mammals are at risk of extinction. Others think it's worse than that. The country with the largest number of endangered species is the United States. Australia ranks second.

Because everything on our planet—plants, animals, humans— is all so interconnected, the final consequences of what climate change is doing to our world are hard to predict. But they are not likely to be good. We are facing the destruction of animals and plants on a scale not seen since the long-running reign of the dinosaurs ended so abruptly tens of millions of years ago. As the dominant species today, humans have thrived so far, tripling our numbers in less than a century. But the costs of our development are not going to be felt just by other species. Klaus Töpfer, who heads the United Nations Environment Program, has warned that the changes global warming is bringing to our weather, and the damage it is doing to habitats, flora and fauna, will also cause massive suffering for humanity. Lives will be lost, are already being lost; our health will suffer; and our financial circumstances will be seriously affected. Nowhere will be immune. No one will be safe. Whether you're in the UK, the United States or the former USSR, it is time to batten down the hatches—the storm is coming.

CHAPTER FOUR

HOW WILL GLOBAL WARMING AFFECT ME?

Late in the summer of 2003, federal officials made a disturbing announcement. During the previous week, an unprecedented number of cases of West Nile virus, a killer disease that had suddenly appeared in the United States just four years earlier, had been diagnosed. The officials warned that as many as half a million Americans could be infected by the end of the year. Later that same day, Hurricane Isabel struck the east coast, leaving fifteen people dead, three-and-a-half million without electricity, and an estimated one billion dollar clean-up bill. Just weeks earlier, the United States had been ravaged by a record-breaking 300 twisters in a single week.

Exactly one year later, a series of even more horrifying events was unfolding across the globe. Four hurricanes swept across the Caribbean and hit Florida and other parts of the United States in rapid succession, leaving hundreds dead and tens of billions of dollars in property damage. At the same time, flash flooding was causing devastation in places as far apart as the Philippines, the UK, southwest China, northern India and Bangladesh, while typhoons were ravaging Japan and Taiwan.

Think these events are unconnected? Think again. More extreme weather and the spread of disease can be clearly linked to global warming.

The effects of global warming are not confined to the changes to our weather and our flora and fauna outlined in previous chapters. People will suffer, too.

Although you may not be aware of it, global warming is already affecting you. It will intrude into your life ever more forcibly—and uncomfortably—as each year passes. Experts say global warming will be with us for decades and even centuries, leaving a bitter inheritance for our children, and our children's children. The less we do about it now, the worse things will be for future generations.

The changes to our climate and weather patterns described earlier, including an increase in the number of extreme weather events such as heat waves, heavy rainstorms and flooding, are already making their presence felt. In fact, the list of ways in which global warming is set to threaten Americans and their way of life is almost endless. Most of these changes will hit us where it hurts most—our health and our wallets.

OUR HEALTH

The changes to America's climate and environment will have a significant effect on people's health. For a start, many experts predict that the increase in extreme weather events, including floods, storms and heat waves, will result in more deaths, injuries and diseases. The greater frequency and severity of heat waves is a particular concern, with the most vulnerable being children, the elderly and those who live in cities and other urban areas, which are often hotter than rural landscapes. Others susceptible to heat waves include people on medications that affect their body's ability to regulate its own temperature and those with respiratory or cardiovascular problems. Catastrophes such as the 15,000 deaths in France caused by record temperatures during the 2003 summer pose a growing threat to America, too.

Storm Clouds Gathering?

More severe storms are also forecast—in fact, their frequency has already increased in recent years. According to Kirsty Duncan and other experts from the Intergovernmental Panel on Climate Change, such storms present a particular problem because "it is difficult to predict where these storms will occur and to identify vulnerable populations." Duncan and her colleagues noted that in one recent year alone, severe storms caused 600 deaths and almost 4,000 injuries in the United States. Thunderstorms can also bring on asthma attacks in some sufferers.

Floods are the most common natural disaster in the United States, claiming 150 lives each year. As shown in chapter two, global warming will make the problem much worse, increasing both the frequency and severity of floods. Victims of such disasters are at risk of post-traumatic stress disorder and depression, while flooding can also result in exposure to toxic wastes, sewage, pesticides and other substances harmful to our health.

Some experts are also convinced that global warming could make hurricanes more intense and powerful. If the four that made landfall in the United States in 2004 with such devastating effect are a taste of what's to come, the future looks bleak indeed.

But it is the less explosive changes to our climate that could have the most far-reaching consequences for your health. Wherever you live, the ongoing changes to your weather are causing the spread of diseases such as West Nile virus, more stress-related disorders and an increase in respiratory illnesses such as asthma.

Disease Alert: West Nile Virus

Since 1999, an alarming new health threat has hit the country. West Nile virus often shows no recognizable symptoms in humans, but in some cases can still develop into life-threatening illnesses such as meningitis (inflammation of the spinal cord) or encephalitis (inflammation of the brain). There is no specific treatment for West Nile virus and no vaccine to prevent it. The virus is transmitted to humans by mosquitoes that have bitten infected birds, and is related to St. Louis encephalitis, a strain of encephalitis already occurring in North America and also transmitted by mosquitoes.

Unlike St. Louis encephalitis, though, not a single case of West Nile virus had ever been reported in the Western Hemisphere, being primarily found in far-away Asia, the Middle East and Africa.

In 1999, all of that changed. Instead of cases cropping up in Uganda, Egypt or Israel, outbreaks were suddenly reported in New York, New Jersey and Connecticut.

"At first, I don't think we took it all that seriously—after all, everything happens in New York, right?" recalled Brooklyn resident Diane Ormrod, an executive with an advertising agency in Manhattan. "Then the authorities started spraying parts of the city—Staten Island and other places—with insecticide, and I realized something was up. Not long after that, an open-air concert I'd been planning on seeing was canceled because they'd temporarily closed Central Park. And when a neighbor told me that an elderly woman living a few blocks away had died, I knew we were facing a serious problem."

By the end of 2000, authorities had reported 83 cases of West Nile virus in these three states, resulting in 9 deaths. By 2002, the virus had spread to 40 states, with almost 4,000 cases and 246 deaths recorded that year alone. By then the Centers for Disease Control and Prevention (CDC), a federal agency, was acknowledging that "the continued expansion of West Nile virus in the United States indicates that it is permanently established in the Western Hemisphere." In other words, West Nile virus is here to stay. Ominously, they were also referring to it as an epidemic.

While there is no consensus on why the virus spread to North America, many experts and environmental groups are increasingly sure climate change is to blame. In an interview in late 2002, Dr. William H. Schlesinger, a professor of biogeochemistry at Duke University, linked diseases like malaria, yellow fever, dengue fever, St. Louis encephalitis and West Nile virus. Noting that all are spread by the mosquito, which needs wet places and a reasonably warm climate to complete its life cycle, he concluded that "any degree of global warming that extends the area of the globe conducive to that life cycle increases the potential for the rapid spread of these kinds of viruses." The CDC has also weighed in on the issue, confirming that "warmer and wetter weather will likely increase the breeding of rodents and insects that spread disease."

The Bugs Are Back

Experts like Dr. Paul Epstein, a specialist with the Harvard School of Public Health, have for some time been describing climate change as a major threat in terms of the spread of diseases such as malaria and dengue fever. As early as the mid-1990s, he was warning that these changes were already happening. "It's a major wake-up call," he claimed.

Epstein was right. According to several recent studies, global warming is set to bring one of the world's most widespread and lethal diseases, malaria, which kills more than one million people each year and affects a staggering 400–500 million, heading northward into much of the United States.

Malaria epidemics have been experienced in America before. They were common throughout the United States and even as far north as Canada during much of the nineteenth century and even early last century. The disease killed as many as one in ten Americans during some earlier epidemics, and even decimated the ranks of Union soldiers during the Civil War, killing more of their troops than did the bloody battles of Gettysburg, Antietam, Bull Run and Shiloh combined.

The disease was successfully eradicated decades ago through better public health measures and water management (the mosquitoes that carry malaria need still or stagnant water to lay their eggs). Now it is set to re-emerge as global warming makes conditions ever more favorable for malaria to spread. It will require a serious and costly response from authorities to prevent it from harming a new generation of Americans. A few cases have already been reported here since the 1990s.

Lyme Disease

Mosquitoes aren't the only bug on the horizon. Lyme disease has become the most common vector-borne illness in America. Passed on to humans bitten by ticks infected with the *Borrelia burgdorferi* bacterium, it is believed to be spreading throughout the United States and even into parts of Canada. While opinions vary on how many cases have occurred so far, the Lyme Disease Network, a not-for-profit group devoted to raising awareness of the problem, believes it to be "one of the fastest growing infectious diseases in the United States." Certainly, reports of the disease have increased exponentially during the past two decades, with thousands of new cases identified each year. The Lyme Disease Network claims that upward of one million Americans have already been infected. The disease often causes flu-like symptoms or a rash, and can usually be treated effectively with antibiotics. Because of its similarity to other illnesses and difficulties detecting it in our bloodstream (bacteria often hide away after entering our bodies), diagnosis is not always easy. Unfortunately, untreated cases can result in arthritis-like symptoms or serious disorders of the nervous system. In spite of ongoing research and monitoring of the disease, it is unclear how fast and far it will spread.

Other less common tick-borne diseases affecting North America include ehrlichiosis and Rocky Mountain Spotted Fever, which ironically is hardly ever found in the Rocky Mountains, being far more common in the Southeast, particularly North Carolina and Oklahoma. While further research is needed to assess how global warming is affecting the incidence of either disease, it is widely believed that changes to our weather are making them more widespread. Both diseases can require hospitalization, and are known to be fatal in some cases.

Those Dirty Rats

In May 1993, a mystery disease that was killing residents of the Four Corners area of the Southwest had health officials worried.

The unidentified illness had its victims coughing and struggling for breath, ending in death by respiratory failure. Initial laboratory tests didn't help, showing only that none of the suspected causes (including the bubonic plague) were to blame. Still baffled, authorities launched a major joint operation to solve the problem, involving the federal CDC Special Pathogens Branch, state health departments, the Indian Health Service and the Navajo Nation.

What they discovered surprised them. The illness was eventually diagnosed as hantavirus pulmonary syndrome (HPS), a disease carried by rodents, especially the deer mouse. It seems that the unusually wet weather had caused a spike in the rodent population, which often thrives in such conditions, thus causing the outbreak of a disease virtually unknown in North America—and one that is fatal in 40 percent of cases. By late 2002, over 300 cases had been reported, and 125 people had died. The disease had been found in at least 31 states, as well as Canada and Latin America. Many experts are convinced that HPS and other illnesses borne by rodents are being spread by global warming, which is creating the warmer and often wetter conditions for rats and mice populations to grow even further, thus increasing human-rodent contact.

Something Fishy about the Water

Although most Americans have access to safe, treated public water supplies, even the most developed countries are not immune from water-borne diseases. Scientists from the Intergovernmental Panel on Climate Change agree that the temperature increases, longer summers and increased precipitation associated with global warming will cause outbreaks of cryptosporidiosis, or "crypto," a diarrheal disease that lives in the intestines and is highly resistant to chlorine disinfection and other water treatments. In 1993, nearly half a million cases and 54 deaths resulted from an outbreak of crypto in Milwaukee's water supply, and in recent years it has established itself as one of the most common water-borne diseases in the country. In Canada, recent tests found it in 3.5 percent of treated water supplies. Although most people recover within two weeks of feeling ill, the disease can become life-threatening for those with weakened immune systems, such as people with HIV/AIDS. As yet, there is no effective treatment for crypto. Giardia, which like crypto is an intestinal parasitic illness, also appears to be on the rise due to global warming.

If it isn't what you drink that hurts you, it could well be what you eat. The warming of oceans and coastal areas during recent El Niño weather cycles will leave a sour taste in some seafood lovers' mouths. Toxic organisms such as red tides—or harmful algal blooms—appear to be thriving in warmer marine water. These organisms can cause shellfish poisoning, with a number of fatal outbreaks reported during the past two decades. Because of global warming, many experts fear worse is to come. Meanwhile, at least one study has found that the effects of climate change on food quality, particularly imported food, will result in more frequent outbreaks of viral, parasitic and bacterial diseases. Currently, diseases transmitted through food cause 76 million illnesses, over 300,000 hospitalizations and 5,000 deaths each year in the United States alone. Global warming seems set to make these worrying statistics even worse.

Take a Deep Breath

"Climate change increases smog," warned IPCC author Kirsty Duncan and her colleagues in 2001. Not only that, but it could increase the levels of other pollutants in the air, too. These changes will certainly affect our health, although to what extent is not yet clear. What we do know is that more than 100 million Americans already live in areas that fail to meet air quality standards for one or more pollutants, a situation few would want to see deteriorate further.

Smog is a particular concern. Known to most as the yellowish haze visible above many cities during summer, it is formed just above the earth's surface from sunlight reacting to the presence of vehicle exhaust fumes or industrial pollutants such as ground-level ozone. Scientists have discovered that global warming is contributing to an increase in such ground-level ozone. This means more smog, which unleashes a whole host of respiratory and pulmanory problems even in healthy adults, although children, the elderly, and those with existing conditions such as asthma and emphysema are most at risk.

Higher levels of acidic aerosols such as nitrogen dioxide, sulfur dioxide and sulfates also cause respiratory illness, with children again being particularly vulnerable. Climate change increases such acidic pollution. It can also raise the level of fine particulates, another form of atmospheric pollution that causes various respiratory illnesses, brings on asthma attacks and even contributes to cardiopulmanory disease and lung cancer. Millions of Americans will be put at risk by such changes.

THE ECONOMY

Predicting the impact global warming will have on our wallets and on the economy in general is no easy task. Forecasts vary about how much the weather will change. While we know that hotter and in some cases wetter weather will occur, it is hard to gauge precisely how much our climate will change and which locations will be most affected. The extent of climate change will depend largely on how quickly and comprehensively we respond to the problem and tackle the issue of our ever-increasing greenhouse gas emissions. Because of this, predicting its economic impact is difficult.

While the big picture remains opaque, research on different sectors of our economy suggests that we will face a long list of likely costs and disruptions in areas as diverse as our water and energy supplies, health costs, insurance premiums, agriculture and even sports and tourism. Regional differences will also emerge.

Insurance Angst

One sector where solid facts and figures can be found is in the insurance business. Global warming is a pressing concern for the industry. Experts agree that losses caused by extreme weather events are already increasing, and have been doing so for at least 30 years. Such losses range from property and crop damage to a marked decline in business productivity resulting from storms, floods and other bad weather. According to reinsurance giant Munich Re, between the 1950s and the 1990s the annual cost of such events rose in real terms from $4 billion to $40 billion. By 2004, that had jumped still further to $60 billion, an inflation-adjusted increase of 1,500 percent over the past 50 years.

In 2003, the worst insured losses were reported in the United States, where tornadoes alone cost insurers in excess of $3 billion. Costs incurred in the United States the previous year included serious damage caused by "a spectacular series of tornadoes, persistent droughts and heat waves, which caused severe damage to agriculture, and devastating forest fires . . . heavy storms and floods along the entire Pacific Coast and the worst snow storms in living memory at Christmas in the Midwest and on the East Coast." By early 2005, the numbers had become worse still. Munich Re declared 2004 the world's "costliest natural disaster year ever for the insurance industry," with losses of $40 billion even before the devastating tsunami that struck South Asia in late December, leaving a death toll of more than 200,000 in its wake. The cyclones that hit the United States, the Caribbean and Japan in 2004 alone generated insured losses of more than $35 billion. Again, Munich Re blamed the increase in extreme weather events on global warming.

If that isn't bad enough, what is now clear is that the worst is yet to come. Insurance losses are set to increase even more dramatically as time goes by. Munich Re recently warned that, as extreme weather events become increasingly common, the large losses of recent years will simply be "a glimpse into the future." The company went on to predict that the economic cost of climate change on the insurance industry will eventually reach a staggering $300 billion *each and every year.* "Losses will continue their sharp upward trend . . . [resulting in] adjustments of insurance prices and conditions," the company announced.

That means many of us will pay more for insurance. In recent years, many insurers were hurt by the increase in extreme weather events, as global warming took most of them by surprise. Now that the industry has woken up to these huge changes, it is already passing on the costs to consumers. For most insurers, it's either that, or risk going bankrupt when another disaster strikes. No company wants to join the fifty or so other American insurers that have become insolvent during the past three decades as a result of insurance payouts for natural disasters.

Insurance firms are also becoming more wary about what they will actually cover. Already, the public sector is heavily involved, with the U.S. government providing flood insurance to residential and small-scale commercial enterprises. Ultimately, this means the taxpayer is liable for the increased risks to private property caused by global warming.

The Rural Picture—Funny Farms and Forest Fires

Global warming will cause some unusual changes to the agricultural sector. Some regions, particularly in the south and east of the country, will suffer, with grain yields set to fall due to drought and higher temperatures. In the northern United States and parts of Canada, though, warmer weather could result in a longer growing season, meaning that production of wheat and other crops will increase. That's potentially good news for an industry worth over $500 billion annually, particularly in light of the overwhelmingly pessimistic forecasts for agriculture in many other parts of the world.

But before you start celebrating our lucky escape, consider this: the U.S. agricultural sector is so large and vulnerable to so many external variables that firm conclusions are extremely difficult to make. "Developing the ability to confidently estimate the impacts of climate change on agriculture is critically important. Unfortunately, we are a long way from having such a capability," explained the experts from the Environmental Protection Agency in a recent report. What's more, other problems such as smog, water shortages, pest infestations and changes in the range of diseases affecting crops and livestock only add to the uncertainty. According to some estimates, the increase in ground-level ozone alone is already causing crop damage of $1–5 billion a year.

Given these doubts and the serious consequences of potentially being wrong, the EPA has cautioned against any complacency. "If vigorous efforts to better understand and prepare for potentially severe impacts are delayed, the nation may face a future time-, resource-, ecological-, and policy-crunch of monumental proportions," it warned.

As with agriculture, predictions for the forestry sector are problematic. Again, regional variations are predicted, with water shortages and more forest fires predicted to cause problems for the forestry sector in the Southeast and possibly elsewhere, and some possible expansion of commercial forestry in the North and at higher altitudes.

Hot in the City

"Deaths from heat waves in large cities could double over the next twenty years." That was the stark message from Godwin Obasi, head of the World Meteorological Organization, during a major United Nations conference back in November 2000. Already, as many as 1,500 people die from heat waves in America's 15 biggest cities each year. Could it really double by 2020?

Yes, it could. Cities are particularly vulnerable to heat waves because built-up areas of buildings and streets absorb and trap heat, which can amplify temperatures, making them higher than in the surrounding countryside or smaller towns (which, incidentally, explains why you can find so few New Yorkers in Manhattan on summer weekends, but meet plenty of them in the less urban, cooler parts of Long Island). This phenomenon, known as the "urban heat island effect," will certainly become even more apparent as global warming continues to make its presence felt. Such heat waves will strain our hospital systems and result in increased health costs.

Heat waves will also require more air conditioning, which means higher energy bills during the summer months. Ironically, while using your air conditioner more regularly, or buying a more powerful unit, will help deal with the immediate problem of higher temperatures, it will also result in greater electricity demand— which in the long run will increase global warming still further. Running more air conditioning will also place greater pressure on the electricity network, which may experience more power outages. This in turn will bring about more heat-related illnesses and mortalities, strain emergency services and hospitals, and almost certainly reduce the productivity of those blue- and white-collar workers affected.

The severe winter storms that ravaged eastern Canada and the northeast of the United States in 1998 provide an example of the economic losses extreme weather can bring. The storms affected transmission lines and other electricity infrastructure, cutting power to over five million people. Forty-five Canadians and Americans died. The disaster cost the two countries $5 billion in direct damage, and countless more in loss of economic productivity (one-fifth of Canada's entire workforce was unable to get to work during the crisis). While such cold weather is actually less likely with climate change, heat waves, floods and other equally damaging extreme weather events are far more probable.

So, Where Did You Spend Your Vacation?

When Christine Beggins and her college friends decided to take a winter break, a snowboarding vacation in Colorado seemed like a wonderful idea. "We'd been wanting to take a trip together for months, and thought this would be a great experience," she recalled.

The group found a good deal on last-minute flights and accommodations over the Internet, and was at the resort four days later.

The only problem was, there wasn't enough snow. "We arrived only to find the season hadn't really gotten started, and none of the slopes were any good. The guide I'd looked up online had said it was usually in full swing weeks earlier, so we'd just assumed it would be okay. It felt like we'd wasted our time and money."

Christine and her friends aren't the only ones to have been disappointed in recent years. Several studies have predicted shorter seasons for many of the world's ski and snowboarding meccas due to global warming, particularly those resorts situated at lower altitudes. In some cases, the average season could shrink by a month or more. Such a change would be bad news for many local businesses. According to the U.S. Global Change Research Program, the loss of 10 to 20 percent of ski season days in New Hampshire alone would cost the local economy up to $84 million in income each year. Snowmaking machines, which some resorts increasingly rely on to make up for nature's shortfall, might not provide a long-term solution. "Snowmaking machines are gluttons for water, a resource that may be in short supply in the next 25 years," warned Dr. Nancy Kete of the World Resources Institute (WRI), a Washington, D.C.–based research organization.

That's not all. According to the WRI, other tourist spots could be affected by the retreat of the snowline. Montana's Glacier National Park, which had 150 glaciers in 1850, will have none by 2030. And if you enjoyed the 2002 Winter Olympics in Salt Lake City, be warned; the WRI also fears that global warming will threaten the success of future games, because the rapid loss of snow in many areas could limit the choice of where to host it, meaning future spectacles might not be as good.

It isn't just our winter skiing industry that will be affected. The impact of global warming on flora and fauna will affect a region's income from tourists seeking thrills as diverse as scuba diving, hiking, recreational fishing, and even golfing, sailing and hunting. Not all these changes will be bad; some could even generate more revenues, particularly from recreational activities that rely on warm weather. Nevertheless, the changes seem certain to cause problems for the tourism industry. An increase in extreme events such as floods, forest fires and heat waves will hurt some tourist destinations. Ongoing sea-level rise and coastal erosion is also set to make its presence felt, especially when one considers that 85 percent of tourist revenues are earned by coastal states. For instance, one study estimates that preserving America's major recreational beaches from sea-level rise will cost as much as $21 billion. Such challenges are obviously worrying for an industry that already generates around $500 billion in global revenues each year, particularly as the United States is currently one of the world's most popular destinations.

Slip Sliding Away?

Loss of tourist dollars due to erosion of our beaches is not the only threat to our coastal areas. "Along the Gulf and Atlantic coasts, a one foot rise in sea level is likely by 2050 and could occur as soon as 2025," the EPA warned recently. It gets worse. "In the next century, a two foot rise is most likely, but a four foot rise is possible and the sea level will probably continue to rise for several centuries," the EPA concluded. The picture is much the same in other coastal areas.

Nearly two hundred million Americans live on or near our coasts. Some large coastal cities such as New York, Boston, Los Angeles and Miami are well protected from the sea, although even these may have to invest in more infrastructure to protect residents from the ocean's incursions. But much of America's coastline is relatively unprotected. According to the Federal Emergency Management Agency (FEMA), 25 percent of homes and other structures within 500 feet of the U.S. coastline and the shorelines of the Great Lakes will fall victim to the effects of erosion within the next 60 years. By 2010, ten thousand buildings will already be lost. Costs to U.S. homeowners will average more than a half billion dollars annually, and additional development in high erosion areas will lead to higher losses. Only half of the homeowners in high erosion areas such as the Atlantic and Gulf coasts currently have flood insurance policies. And insurance rates are likely to rise, with price hikes estimated at 36 to 58 percent if the increasing risks are to be adequately covered. The situation will almost certainly become even worse; a great deal of new property development in Florida and other states is on the coast, so the number of vulnerable properties is increasing.

Water, Water Everywhere?

In the summer of 2002, the worst drought in a generation struck the continental United States, placing half of the country under drought conditions. The water shortage hit farmers hard, with the Department of Agriculture declaring Utah and parts of Arizona, California, Colorado and New Mexico "agricultural disaster areas." Wildfires raged over four million acres, twice the average during the previous decade. Water supplies for residential and industrial uses were threatened and lower lake levels caused serious concerns for electricity generation from hydro-electric power plants. The drought continued a dry spell that had already lasted four years in parts of the West and Southeast. Residents of some towns were fined for watering their lawns and restrictions were even placed on flushing the toilet.

"We're in a desperate situation here," Glen Branch, the water commissioner for Electra, Texas, told a CNN reporter in 2000 following a three-year drought. "Watering your lawn, watering your flower beds is kind of like committing murder," he said. The last major drought in the United States, in the late 1980s, cost the country an estimated $40 billion.

While climate change will increase precipitation in some areas, others, particularly in the south and west of the country, could be left short. This will present a major problem, particularly as the population of many of those states is set to continue growing.

What's more, a shift toward more extreme weather events, including heavy rainfall and storms, will mean that even areas receiving plenty of rainfall will be at risk, as more regular precipitation patterns throughout the year are replaced by too much rain in winter and spring (resulting in flooding), followed by too little rain in summer (which could cause drought).

Even without global warming, the country will face problems resulting from its ever-increasing population. Higher water demands in the United States are projected to increase supply costs by nearly $14 billion within the next three decades. With global warming affecting the water supply, meeting that additional demand will be a problem, and seems certain to hike up costs even further. As consumers and taxpayers, we will bear the burden of these additional costs.

Counting All the Costs

As well as the cost implications for our water and energy supplies, health spending, insurance premiums, agriculture and tourism outlined above, there are also a host of other economic perils that could result from climate change, but that are as yet difficult to predict or measure. To take just one example, consider the case of the heavy storms and flooding that struck California in early 2005. While it is not possible to say that this specific event was caused by climate change, experts do believe that an increase in this type of weather is happening. Obviously, the torrential downpours that hit California had some serious direct implications in terms of property damage and even loss of life. But what about all the other, less obvious economic consequences that could be added to this? For instance, what if this weather led to some high-profile sporting event, such as a college football bowl game, being postponed? While television audiences might be disappointed at the interruption of their regular weekend viewing, the implications go much further than that. For instance, what impact does the postponement of a major sporting event have on advertising revenues, or on television viewing figures? How does this affect a network's income? And in the longer term, does the host city's sudden reputation as a place that's vulnerable to extreme weather mean event organizers may be less inclined to hold major concerts or sporting fixtures there in the future? What sort of impact does this have on the local economy, from food, drink or merchandise sales to parking lot use and even hotel bookings? Such indirect financial implications are almost impossible to measure, but are probably far from negligible.

REGIONAL IMPACTS

While the threats to people's health and economic well-being from climate change will be significant wherever they live, some of the specific effects will almost certainly vary depending on the location. Although precise changes can be hard to predict, it is already clear that every region and even sub-region will face its own unique set of problems and challenges. Some of the key challenges each region of the United States may face during the next 20 years include:

West Coast and Rocky Mountains. Rapid population growth and global warming will cause energy and water shortages that will affect domestic and industrial supplies as well as the agricultural and hydro-energy sectors. Winter tourism will suffer due to higher temperatures, causing job losses in this sector.

Southwest. An increased risk of drought, heat waves, flash floods and water shortages represent key threats to people's health and the region's economy.

Midwest. An increase in the number of droughts will affect agriculture. Increased air pollution and disease risks are likely.

Great Lakes. Water supply and lake levels will decline and hydropower production will fall due to changes in rainfall patterns. More heat waves are likely.

Northeast. Coastal erosion will threaten some communities. More heat waves will occur, and vector-borne diseases will increase. Air quality will deteriorate, with significant impacts on people's health. Winter tourism will suffer.

Southeast, Gulf and Mid-Atlantic. Flooding, sea-level rise and coastal erosion are predicted. Agricultural productivity will be affected. An increase in vector-borne diseases, more extreme weather events such as storms, floods and possibly even hurricanes and tornadoes will also seriously impact the region's population. Tourism will suffer from beach erosion.

GLOBAL CONSEQUENCES

While climate change is creating many problems for the United States, the good news, if you can call it that, is that it could be worse.

You could be living somewhere else.

Much of the world is set to suffer even more than America. The reason for this is simple; when it comes to tackling global warming, a country's level of economic development makes a big difference. All countries will face problems and economic costs. But those boasting more developed economies, skills and infrastructure—such as the United States, Japan, Germany and Britain—will have the tools to deal with it more effectively. Here's what different parts of the world have to look forward to.

Africa

For Africa, global warming will make a bad situation worse.

"The African continent is particularly vulnerable to the impacts of climate change because of factors such as widespread poverty, recurrent droughts, inequitable land distribution, and overdependence on rain-fed agriculture," explained African expert Abdelkader Allali and his colleagues from the Intergovernmental Panel on Climate Change in a report published in 2001.

Most of Africa is already in trouble. Nearly half the population subsists below the poverty line. Disease is rampant, with malaria killing almost 1 million Africans annually, and with 30 million people with HIV/AIDS—three-quarters of the world total—living there. Millions face starvation and still more dwell in countries that are at war either with their neighbors or themselves. Land once used to grow crops is being lost to the encroaching deserts. Water resources are becoming increasingly scarce, a problem set to reach a crisis point as Africa's population jumps from an estimated 750 million today to over 2 billion by 2050.

While Africa will experience many of the same effects from global warming as will North America, including higher temperatures and more extreme weather events (although less rainfall in many areas), its ability to adapt to these changes is far more limited. In most of Africa, health services are less able to deal with outbreaks of new diseases, properties are more vulnerable to storms or floods and coastal areas are less well protected against sea-level rise.

"If carbon pollution is left unchecked, climate change will have a pervasive effect on life in Africa. It will threaten the people, animals and natural resources," Dr. Paul Desanker, a professor at the University of Virginia, warned participants at a major UN conference held in South Africa in 2002.

Asia

Asia is also extremely vulnerable to climate change, although the effects will differ markedly across the region. Central Asia will suffer the most dramatic effects. Temperatures that often average a sweltering 100°F will jump by a further 10°F. Droughts and famine will become even more common. India and parts of Russia will also experience even more significant temperature hikes. Meanwhile, many large cities, such as Tokyo, are already feeling the urban heat island effect and are experiencing far greater increases in temperature than non-urban areas, as well as the host of health concerns that often accompany such increases. Additionally, the range of some tropical diseases is expected to spread northward into parts of Asia that were previously unaffected. Drought and growing pressures on water supply and availability are also forecast.

But it is Asia's coastal areas that are perhaps most at risk. More than half of Asia's population, some 1.7 billion people, lives in low-lying coastal areas. Across the region, from India to Indonesia, sea-level rise and an increase in storms and flooding could have disastrous consequences. In Bangladesh, the three-feet rise in sea level predicted by some scientists to occur this century would mean nearly one-fifth of the entire country disappears under water, displacing nearly 20 million people. An estimated 70 million Chinese would be similarly affected.

Canada

Like the United States, Canada will have a greater ability to adapt to climate change than will many other countries. It will probably need it. According to the Intergovernmental Panel on Climate Change, heat waves will cause a significant rise in mortalities in some of Canada's major cities, with up to 3,000 additional heat-related deaths forecast each year for Montreal, Toronto and Ottawa. There may be fewer deaths from extreme cold weather and winter storms, though. Air quality could become a serious issue, especially in urban areas, with a particular problem for Canadians being ground-level ozone, which can cause various respiratory illnesses. Some vector-borne diseases, including various strains of encephalitis, could also become more widespread.

In British Columbia and on the Atlantic coast, sea-level rise will threaten coastal properties, and more frequent flooding will occur in some areas. The Canadian prairies and parts of Ontario will see an increase in droughts, although their effect on agriculture may be offset by longer growing seasons, the extension of agriculture in the north and crop yield gains in Quebec. Fire risks will also increase in parts of Canada. Arctic areas will change markedly, with glacial melting increasing and local communities profoundly affected.

Europe

This region also has the advantage of being economically developed. Unfortunately, it is also constrained by its high population density and relatively few natural resources, which could limit its room to maneuver in facing the challenges ahead.

Flooding, which is already a common occurrence throughout Europe, will become an increasing preoccupation, especially given the continent's long coastline and vulnerability to sea-level rise. One recent report suggested that in Britain alone, five million people, and much of the country's farmland, will soon be under threat. According to some estimates, the costs associated with a major disaster could run to hundreds of billions of dollars.

In southern Europe, fire risks, drought and water shortages will become increasingly common, and will have a pronounced effect on agriculture. Northern Europe may well experience an overall increase in agricultural productivity, however. Meanwhile, in central Europe, higher temperatures will result in glacial melting, significantly impacting local communities, not to mention winter tourism. An increase in the number and severity of heat waves will also affect summer tourist destinations and, more importantly, cause more heat-related illness and deaths, particularly in urban areas and in southern Europe. Malaria and some other vector-borne diseases are also set to spread into the region.

Latin America and the Caribbean

Less rainfall and drought in many areas, including much of Central America and western South America, will cause problems for the tens of millions of people who rely on agriculture for their income and even their survival. Tropical diseases such as malaria are set to become more widespread, expanding into much of South

America. Higher temperatures in urban areas such as Mexico City will worsen pollution and have a negative impact on human health.

In the Caribbean, sea-level rise will threaten many small island countries. Even a minor change would erode the coasts, potentially devastating the tourist industry, one of the region's largest sources of income.

Some scientists now believe global warming will make hurricanes both more intense and more devastating. If the prediction is correct, the Caribbean and parts of Central and South America will be in for a difficult time. Few would wish for a repetition of the devastation wrought by Hurricane Mitch, which caused at least 9,000 deaths in Honduras and Nicaragua in 1998, and caused the loss of 70 percent of Nicaragua's gross national product.

Oceania

For Pacific Island countries, global warming could spell disaster. For some, it will, quite literally, mean the end. With sea-level rise, islands are actually beginning to disappear. Take Kiribati, for instance (the locals pronounce it "Kiribas," although, as they point out, how they say it might not matter soon). The tiny island nation is already suffering from coastal erosion and storms as the surrounding ocean gradually rises. If the trend continues, much of it will be claimed by the sea. Other island countries, such as Tuvalu and the Marshall Islands, face similar problems. For them, global warming is a matter of survival. At the very least, the loss of beaches and erosion will severely damage their tourist industry, which for many is the only major source of income.

Australia and New Zealand, the two "giants" of the South Pacific, are expected to suffer from less dire—though no less real—problems. Australia is vulnerable to temperature and rainfall changes, as much of the country is already dominated by deserts and relatively unproductive land. An anticipated drop in rainfall in many areas will affect water supplies and agriculture, with potentially serious consequences for the economy. Droughts and wildfires are far more likely, and are already a significant problem. In 2002, drought and dry weather caused the usually lucrative wheat crop yield to decline by almost 60 percent. It also slashed as much as one percent from the country's expected economic growth figures, caused hundreds of bushfires in and around Sydney, and forced Melbourne to impose water use restrictions for the first time in 20 years.

New Zealand, with a more temperate climate, may suffer less than its neighbors, although parts of the country are expected to suffer from a drop in rainfall, particularly in eastern areas. This will have consequences for water resources and the agriculture and forestry sectors, which are both key parts of its economy.

IS THERE STILL HOPE?

It all makes for a pretty grim picture. Reading about the heat waves, floods, disease, pollution, droughts, water shortages and slew of other problems we can expect in the near future, you could be forgiven for wondering if it's worth trying to deal with the problem at all.

It is, but first, some encouraging news; not all the changes will be bad. Higher levels of carbon dioxide means many plants will grow faster. Combined with warmer weather and more rainfall, this change means the United States could see benefits for its agricultural sector, especially in the north—although it could also harm some ecosystems (see chapter three).

Because of the warmer weather, tourism could get a boost in some areas, and winters will generally be milder. More important still, the number of deaths and illnesses resulting from extremely cold weather and winter storms could decline.

Such changes to the climate could offer economic benefits, too. Combating global warming, and adapting to the changes it brings, has the potential to bring income opportunities in high-technology areas such as the renewable energy field, something that an industrialized country like the United States could benefit from.

In spite of this, most experts agree that the potential risks and problems associated with climate change far outweigh its benefits.

But there is hope. According to the Intergovernmental Panel on Climate Change, the future is in our hands. While we cannot completely prevent global warming from happening now that it has begun, we can influence how fast and how far the process goes, and how much harm it does.

In 2001, the Panel's experts publicized a range of future scenarios, which are based on how we respond to the problem. In one scenario—that optimistically assumes far-reaching initiatives and pro-active responses—temperatures in North America are predicted to rise by as little as two degrees Fahrenheit during the course of the next 100 years. In another, less optimistic scenario, the Panel can imagine an America where temperatures have increased in some places by an alarming 16 degrees. Clearly, the differences between the two possibilities, and what they mean both for us and our children, are enormous.

As the world's biggest polluter, the United States holds the key to solving the problem. The good news is that each of us can contribute to solving this problem. We can all make a difference. Surprisingly, many of the changes will be easy and quite painless. Some will save or even make you money. And all will help ensure that it is the Panel's dream scenario, rather than its nightmare vision, that becomes a reality.

The second half of this book will explain what is already being done to deal with global warming, and what needs to happen next. It sets out solutions for government, big business, local communities and, most important, each of us as individuals, to deal with this looming challenge.

CHAPTER FIVE

WHAT IS BEING DONE TO TACKLE THE PROBLEM?

"The earth's well-being is an issue important to America—and it's an issue that should be important to every nation and in every part of the world. My Administration is committed to a leadership role on the issue of climate change. We recognize our responsibility and we will meet it, at home, in our hemisphere, and in the world."

—President George W. Bush, 2001

On the face of it, President Bush's comments could easily be interpreted as a serious response to a serious problem. With the evidence for climate change and its destructive powers accumulating by the day, the President's pledge to play a key role was without doubt the right thing to do. The leader of the world's most powerful country—and biggest global polluter—had made a commitment to meet his responsibilities. What's more, he had challenged the rest of the world to do the same, sounding what seemed like a call to arms to others to take the issue seriously, too.

Several years on, those words sound hollow. The promise has not been kept. The United States remains the world's worst polluter, and its emissions continue to rise. In spite of the massive evidence of the need to cut our greenhouse gas emissions dramatically and rapidly, America persists in doing the very opposite, with our use of fossil fuels continuing to increase, and emissions actually climbing by an average of 1.5 percent every year since Bush's pledge in 2001. According to estimates from the U.S. Energy Information Administration published in December 2004, the United States produces seven *billion* tons of carbon dioxide and other greenhouse gases each year—more than China, India and Russia combined. On current trends, this will grow by as much as one-third within just 15 years.

Not that the rest of the world is doing much better. Greenhouse gas emissions continue to spiral upwards in all but a handful of countries around the world. In many nations, emissions are rising even more quickly than they are in the United States (although to be fair, other countries' emissions were far, far lower to begin with, and still are). While scientists are warning that we must cut the use of fossil fuels by two-thirds in the coming years, exploitation of oil, coal and gas around the world continues to rise. Since 1970, consumption of these fuels has doubled. By 2030, it is expected to double once again. That's a recipe for disaster, not safety. Meanwhile, the only international treaty offering any hope of genuine global progress to combat this massive threat, the Kyoto Protocol, remains the subject of bitter divisions between the United States and a small "coalition of the unwilling" on the one hand, and Europe and most of the rest of the world on the other.

With the evidence for global warming now so overwhelming, a visitor to our planet could be forgiven for wondering just what we are all playing at. Are we really ignoring this threat, preferring to keep our heads in the sand rather than face up to such a major problem?

Actually, no: while nowhere near enough is yet happening, some action is already underway at the international, national and even local levels both to slow down the rising concentration of greenhouse gases that are responsible for global warming and to adapt to a world that is already feeling the phenomenon's effects. For at least the past 15 years, the international community, individual governments and local communities have been trying to tackle the growing threat. More must be done—a lot more. But a modest start has already been made.

So just what has happened to date, and what is being done right now, to take the heat out of global warming?

THE INTERNATIONAL RESPONSE

Climate change is a global problem. It respects no countries' boundaries or sovereignty. It needs no permission to cross from nation to nation and not even the finest border patrol can keep it out. It does not discriminate and it has no favorites. It spares no one. It is already inflicting itself on the entire planet, regardless of who caused it or is to blame. In short, the climate system is global, and changes to the system will be felt globally, too. This means that what people do about the threat in China or Africa, the pollution that is produced there, and the solutions that are found, will reverberate in, say, the United States and Europe—and vice versa. Some experts like to use a water analogy to describe the situation. They compare our planet to a lifeboat. If one part of the lifeboat starts taking on water, they say, it does not matter if the rest of the timbers have been kept watertight and in tip-top shape—the whole boat will still sink. The lesson from this is clear: either we cooperate at an international level on this planetwide problem, or we will fail to bring the problem under control. Stand together, or we all go under.

The global nature of this threat was actually recognized very early on. The first major international climate conference, held in 1979, sparked public concern over the possibility that our use of fossil fuels was adversely affecting the entire world's climate system. The conference resulted in a series of diplomatic meetings on the matter over the next few years, and by 1988 the United Nations General Assembly—the biggest forum for government-to-government discussion and debate in the world—had decided it was time to pass a resolution on the matter, calling on governments around the world to protect the global climate for present and future generations.

That same year, the UN Environment Program and World Meteorological Organization launched a major new organization charged with tackling the scientific questions head-on. The Intergovernmental Panel on Climate Change (IPCC) was tasked with investigating the matter in-depth, assessing the latest research and providing objective assessments of exactly what, if anything, was happening to the global climate. From the start, the IPCC took its work seriously, marshalling literally thousands of scientists and leading experts in its mission to investigate the science of climate change and figure out just what was really happening. The IPCC had an almost immediate impact on the international diplomatic community, as its scientists soon confirmed the potential seriousness of the threat and supported the case for global action. When the Panel issued its first major report in 1990, it was clear that something close to a consensus was already starting to emerge among the mainstream scientific community. Since then, the evidence has become even more compelling, and the IPCC's language has altered in tone, from expressing more cautious concerns about the "possible" threat in its first report, to increasingly stark warnings of a clear and present danger to our global climate as the years have passed. Even in 1990, though, the scientific community's fears were sufficient to spark serious discussions on the need for a global response to the problem. At a major conference held in Geneva shortly after the IPCC's first report came out, delegates felt sufficiently worried that they decided to call for a global treaty to combat the problem. The UN General Assembly agreed, passing a second resolution that set in motion diplomatic talks aimed at developing such a treaty. The global response had begun.

THE UN CLIMATE TREATY

Discussions started in earnest in early 1991. Following a long-standing tradition of never keeping a title short and memorable when it can be made long and convoluted, the UN established an "Intergovernmental Negotiating Committee for a United Nations Framework Convention on Climate Change"—a tongue twister even by diplomatic standards—as the forum for its negotiations. In spite of being burdened by such a forgettable name, government negotiators took to their work with a creditable zeal, finalizing the terms of a treaty in just 15 months, the mere blink of an eye in the diplomatic world. In May 1992, the new climate change convention was presented at the Rio Earth Summit—a major showcase event that drew dozens of world leaders to discuss climate change and a host of other threats to the world's environment. Governments rapidly signed the new climate treaty, with many ratifying it into law in their national legislative assemblies. Under the terms of the convention, at least 50 countries had to confirm their support by legislating it into their national laws before the treaty could claim the weight of international law. Support for the treaty was so widespread that it reached the 50-country requirement within just 18 months, becoming a legally binding agreement in early 1994.

A decade later, almost every country has joined the consensus, with 189 nations pledging to stand by the treaty and its promise to combat global warming. From major powers such as the United States, Britain, France, Germany, Japan, China, Russia and India, to minnows like Luxembourg, Micronesia and Tuvalu, the climate change convention has secured worldwide support. Few international agreements have been so universally endorsed.

So far, so good. But what, exactly, does the treaty do? What obligations does it impose on the 189 countries that have dutifully signed on the dotted line? And how many of these promises have actually been met?

Firm Foundations

The UN Framework Convention on Climate Change represents a firm first step on the part of the world's governments and the international community in combating global warming. For a start, the treaty recognizes that there is a major problem that governments need to acknowledge and face up to. It establishes a common understanding of the climate change problem and the serious threat it represents. It also agrees that human activities are responsible for an increase in greenhouse gases in the atmosphere, which is in turn resulting in further warming of the planet. It acknowledges the global nature of climate change, and calls for the widest possible cooperation by all countries in framing an international response to the problem. At the same time, though, the convention notes that some countries have contributed more to the problem, particularly those in the West, because of their heavy use of fossil fuels dating back to the Industrial Revolution.

The ultimate aim of the convention, according to the agreed text, is to stabilize the concentrations of greenhouse gases in the atmosphere at a level that will prevent our fossil fuel use from becoming a "dangerous interference" with the climate system. In other words, we should not churn out carbon dioxide and other gases at levels that would change the planet's natural greenhouse effect enough to threaten human development or other life on our planet.

As well as acknowledging the problem and agreeing that it must be prevented, the UN climate treaty also sets out some basic principles for how to approach the problem. These include a specific agreement that while all countries must play a part, the world's wealthiest nations, such as the United States, Japan, Britain and its neighbors in Europe, should take the lead. In addition, the treaty makes it clear that, even if the science is not 100 percent certain, the threat of serious damage to the planet means that precautionary measures are absolutely essential. Lack of full scientific certainty should not be used as an excuse for inaction.

Promises, Promises

The climate convention did more than simply agree on the key aims and principles that should guide the international response to global warming, though. It also contained a series of quite specific commitments and pledges that countries joining the treaty are supposed to implement. These include promises to develop precise policies to combat climate change, to cooperate on developing and sharing technologies such as wind or solar power, to help reduce greenhouse gas emissions and to collaborate in adapting to the changes brought on by climate change. Every country that is a party to the treaty is also obliged to report on its greenhouse gas emissions and to promote educational activities and raise public awareness.

While these pledges were intended for every country that joined the treaty, some other obligations were not. Recognizing that the world's wealthiest countries were better equipped to combat global warming, and had also done more to cause the problem, the convention contained additional commitments for this select group. Under the treaty, 38 countries were asked to take the lead in limiting their greenhouse gas emissions. This group included the world's most industrialized nations, as well as many countries of the former Soviet Union and its satellite states in eastern and central Europe. The climate convention refers to this select group of countries as "Annex I" nations (for the simple reason that they are listed in an annex at the end of the treaty document). A subset of this group, known simply as Annex II countries, took on even stronger obligations. The Annex II group includes only the world's richest 20-odd countries—Canada, the United States, Australia, New Zealand, Japan and the nations of western Europe. These states are expected not only to combat climate change themselves, but to help the 150-plus poorer countries of the Third World do so, too, by providing both technical expertise and financial support. According to the treaty, these struggling developing countries (known as "non–Annex I countries" in UN-speak) should receive financial assistance from the West in the global war against warming. Industrialized nations should also share any suitable new technologies they have developed with their poorer neighbors.

Just Starting Out

While the UN climate treaty was quite an achievement, it really did little more than lay the foundations for future work. For a start, its stated goal of stabilizing greenhouse gas concentrations in the atmosphere at a safe level neglected to make clear what those levels might be—leaving the matter to be resolved at a later time. Even 12 years on, that has yet to happen. And while the treaty made it clear that the world's richest countries should take the lead, it did not try to resolve the thorny question of exactly how much they should do compared with the rest of the world, or how much help they should give their less affluent Third World partners. To be fair, some elements of the deal were deliberately left vague, both because of the scientific uncertainties still existing at the time, and because some countries might not have signed up if the pledges had been too precise. For instance, if negotiators had tried to place a dollar value on how much assistance the West should give the developing world, talks may well have broken down.

Another major shortcoming of the climate change convention was that it did not set any precise goals for how much countries should try to cut their emissions. Fortunately, the treaty required that further meetings should be held on a regular basis to follow up on the agreement, gauge its success and discuss further ways to combat climate change. These annual meetings, known officially as "Conferences of the Parties," instantly became major events in the UN calendar. At the very first Conference in 1995, delegates agreed that they must build on the treaty by setting new targets that would legally oblige countries to reduce their future emissions. A new round of negotiations began immediately. The result, some two-and-a-half years later, was the Kyoto Protocol.

THE KYOTO PROTOCOL

The negotiations that led to the Kyoto Protocol were far from easy. Trying to accommodate the views and wishes of more than 150 countries on an issue as complex and politically charged as climate change was never going to be a straightforward task, especially as it was becoming clear that combating climate change was not going to come cheap. With nations as diverse as the oil-exporting states of the Middle East, the rapidly developing Asian giants such as China and India, the oil-reliant United States, environmentally sympathetic European countries and impoverished nations of Africa all thrown into the mix, it was always going to be difficult to please everyone. The discussions reached a critical point at the third meeting of the Conference of Parties, held in Kyoto, Japan, in late 1997. Success seemed unlikely, and some feared the meeting would break up without an agreement being reached. At the eleventh hour, though, delegates secured a compromise that seemed to satisfy almost everyone.

The deal committed industrialized countries to cut their emissions of carbon dioxide and five other greenhouse gases by 5 percent between 1990 and 2012—an ambitious target. But as a sweetener for those that took on such obligations, the deal offered a lot of leeway and flexibility in how they kept their pledge to reduce emissions. This flexibility allowed governments not only to take credit for cutting emissions in their own countries, but also to cooperate with other countries, and be credited for helping others cut their emissions, too. The treaty encouraged a free-market, capitalist-style approach to the problem. The idea behind this was to create a cooperative and flexible approach that would help reduce any financial burden countries might face in meeting their emissions targets—after all, why pay more to achieve your goals if you can do it for less? The three key instruments in the Kyoto pact set up to support this global cooperation were known as the "flexible mechanisms."

A "Flexible" Deal

The first of the three "mechanisms" is known as "emissions trading." In simple terms, it allows countries and companies to trade their "right" to emit greenhouse gases. This "right" to emit greenhouse gases was part of the agreement reached in Kyoto. While industrialized countries pledged to cut their emissions down to a set limit, the deal effectively gave them the right to produce emissions right up to that limit, and to gain financial rewards if they came in under their target. For instance, many eastern European countries saw their economies stagnate in the 1990s, meaning that their emissions of greenhouse gases actually declined as their fossil fuel–consuming factories and power plants reduced their output. In some of these countries, emissions fell by 30 or 40 percent. Thus even though they may not have actively taken measures to reduce emissions, they are likely to end up producing less than the quota set down for them for 2012 when compared with 1990, which means they have emission rights they can sell. On the other hand, countries like Japan or Canada expect to produce more than their allotted share of emissions. A trading scheme therefore allows one country to buy part of another's right to pollute.

A second market-based method that a country can use to reach its Kyoto targets is the "clean development mechanism." Under this approach, industrialized countries can receive credits toward their Kyoto targets by helping poorer developing countries find ways to stop polluting. As an example, policymakers in a developed country such as Germany might discover that it is actually less expensive for them to support a project to prevent emissions in, say, Ghana, than it is to fund the same project back home. Perhaps the labor costs involved in completing a project in Ghana are less than those in Germany, or maybe Ghana might not have introduced some inexpensive plan to cut emissions that has already been implemented in Germany. Whatever the reason, the clean development mechanism basically allows industrialized countries to count the help they provide to the Third World on climate change toward their own emissions targets if it turns out to be cheaper than taking action at home. The end result—a cut in global emissions—would bring exactly the same benefits for the environment;

but the expense for the industrialized country in meeting its Kyoto commitments would be less.

The third method is known as "joint implementation." It works in a similar way to the clean development mechanism, but instead of involving cooperation between rich and poor countries, it involves industrialized countries and former members of the Soviet Union and its satellite states such as Romania, Poland, Estonia and the Ukraine. The scheme makes financial sense because the nations of the former Soviet bloc often have industries that use older technologies and heavily polluting coal-fired power plants. Most of their wealthier neighbors such as Germany, Britain or France have already upgraded their own plants, meaning they have the know-how and skills to do it elsewhere. It is frequently less expensive to upgrade these facilities in the former Soviet bloc than to try to find further emissions reductions in places like Germany or Britain, which are already well on the way to making their power stations and industries less polluting.

This, then, was the deal struck in Kyoto in 1997. Unfortunately, though, much of the fine print about how the pact would work in practice had yet to be figured out. For instance, negotiators still had to agree on precisely how a country's efforts would be judged, and what would happen if it failed to keep its promises. While the world's wealthiest countries, including the United States, had agreed to the deal in principle, none was ready to sign up formally and make the agreement law until these details had been finalized. And that is where things started to unravel.

It soon became more than obvious that, as far as Kyoto was concerned, the devil was in the details. Negotiations on the Protocol's fine print dragged on for more than five years, with negotiators only finishing up their work in 2003. One of the problems was that many diplomats seemed to have very different views of what had been agreed in Kyoto. Naturally, most governments interpreted the deal in a way that suited them and their economic circumstances and interests.

Kyoto's Fatal Flaws

The problem finally came to a head in early 2001 when the Bush administration in the United States rejected it outright.

"The Kyoto Protocol is fatally flawed in fundamental ways," announced President Bush at the time. According to Bush, the Kyoto deal was a bad one for the United States because it only placed obligations on industrialized countries, letting other major polluters like China off scot-free. Meanwhile, the United States would be at an unfair disadvantage economically, as the costs imposed by its efforts to cut its fossil fuel use and develop environmentally friendly forms of energy would hamper its ability to compete with developing countries that had no such obligations to cut their use of tried, tested and cheap sources of energy like coal and gas. Furthermore, Bush argued, the science did not yet justify imposing such targets.

Bush was wrong on all counts. It was his policy, not Kyoto's, that was flawed, his administration that allowed itself to be manipulated and exploited by self-serving friends and big-money donors from the oil and coal industries (for more on this, refer to chapter six). The U.S. rejection of Kyoto is all the more ironic because the treaty is in truth a very American agreement. When the Kyoto Protocol was being negotiated in 1997, American negotiators argued forcefully, and convincingly, that the economic implications of cutting emissions must be accounted for. They reasoned that neither voters nor businesspeople would support a deal that hit them too hard financially. Put simply, the United States wanted a deal that would save money as well as the planet. The result was a Protocol that focused on market-based, cost-effective solutions. Rather than compelling governments to concentrate exclusively on projects that cut emissions in their own countries, it allows them to find the most cost-effective ways possible to reduce emissions anywhere in the world. Much as a multinational company might decide, for instance, that it can find cost savings by having its manufacturing plants in a different country than its call centers, so Kyoto allows countries and companies to manage their costs by taking their emissions cuts offshore. It is just the sort of arrangement that an entrepreneurial nation like the United States would have thrived on.

Instead, the U.S. government turned its back on the treaty, alienating many of its friends in the process. Even Britain, arguably its closest ally, was incensed. While Tony Blair was pledging to continue cutting his country's emissions (and succeeding, so far), his friend George Bush was doing almost exactly the opposite. The decision also caused disquiet in the United States. Even some fellow Republicans, such as Senator John McCain, expressed dismay at the decision.

"Nothing has further alienated the United States from the rest of the world than the Bush administration's dismissal of global climate change," said Ross Gelbspan in 2004. A Pulitzer Prize winner and one of America's most experienced reporters, Gelbspan's comments summed up perfectly the views of almost every other nation—and a good many of his compatriots.

The Bush administration's rejection of the deal has not prevented most other countries from joining the consensus on Kyoto, though. By early 2005, more than 140 nations had signed on the dotted line. This included over 30 industrialized countries or members of the former Soviet bloc that had taken on actual commitments to cut their emissions of greenhouse gases. Table 5.1 shows which industrialized countries joined the treaty and took on commitments, and which rejected it.

So there you have it; dozens in favor, just two against. Only John Howard's conservative government in Australia joined George W. Bush in rejecting the treaty—and even Howard did not take such an extreme position as President Bush (Australia has left the door open on emissions targets and on joining a post-Kyoto treaty). In spite of the Bush administration, then, Kyoto seemed to have almost overwhelming support in the rest of the world. Which begs the question, If the treaty is so bad, why has almost everybody else signed up to it?

The U.S. rejection, though, did raise a problem with Kyoto's fine print. Under the terms of the treaty, Kyoto would only become

Table 5.1

Countries Supporting Kyoto	Countries Against Kyoto
Austria	Australia
Belgium	United States
Britain	
Bulgaria	
Canada	
Czech Republic	
Denmark	
Estonia	
Finland	
France	
Germany	
Greece	
Hungary	
Iceland	
Ireland	
Italy	
Japan	
Latvia	
Lithuania	
Luxembourg	
Netherlands	
New Zealand	
Norway	
Poland	
Portugal	
Romania	
Russian Federation	
Slovakia	
Slovenia	
Spain	
Sweden	
Switzerland	
Ukraine	

legally binding under international law when most of the world's industrialized countries supported it. In an unusual mathematical twist, the deal stipulated that the Protocol would become official only if enough of the world's industrialized countries signed up so that at least 55 percent of that group's total carbon dioxide emissions were represented. This put its supporters in an awkward position, because as the world's biggest polluter, the United States represented a whopping 35 percent of these emissions. Without the United States, almost every other wealthy country would have to agree to join the pact. If this didn't happen, the treaty would never be granted the full force of international law. Kyoto would be dead in the water.

Playing Russian Roulette with the Protocol

Fortunately, almost every other wealthy nation *did* sign up. Most of the major European nations ratified the pact in 2002, while Japan, Canada and a few others joined them shortly after. Attention then focused on Russia—if it came on board, too, then Kyoto would finally become law, imposing legal obligations on every country that had agreed to it. On the other hand, if Russia joined the Americans in rejecting the treaty, then it would be certain that Kyoto would fail. Knowing that it held the Protocol's future in its hands, the Russians refused to commit themselves either way, hoping to extract further concessions and sweeteners from the Europeans, who by this stage desperately wanted to see the Protocol succeed. Throughout 2003 and 2004, Russian officials continued to send mixed signals. In particular, one of President Vladimir Putin's advisers, Andrei Illarionov, caused frequent anguish and alarm in the pro-Kyoto camp with his increasingly scathing comments about the treaty.

Like George Bush, Illarionov seemed to be singularly unimpressed with the deal and its potential impact on his country. Unlike Bush, Illarionov's anti-Kyoto comments could be colorful in the extreme. On one occasion in 2004, his penchant for unusual prose reached new highs (or lows) as he declared the Protocol to be an "economic death sentence" for Russia, even likening it to Auschwitz, the World War II Nazi concentration camp. Fortunately, it became apparent that Illarionov's increasingly extreme views would fail to carry the day. After months of speculation about Russia's intentions, President Vladimir Putin announced in September 2004 that his government would finally ratify the Kyoto Protocol, and the treaty gained official recognition as a legally binding international agreement in February 2005.

Success over Kyoto represented a victory for those advocating an international approach to this global problem; it was also a slap in the face for George Bush. But the victory came at a cost. Without the United States, Kyoto lacks the support of the world's biggest polluter and most powerful nation-state—the country that is arguably the single greatest cause of, and solution to, the climate change threat. Without the United States, Kyoto will simply not have as big an impact.

Beyond Kyoto

Regardless of whether or not the United States does eventually come on board and join the consensus, Kyoto really is just a start, another small step in the right direction. Many more such steps are needed. Even if the Protocol is fully implemented, more ambitious targets for reining in our fossil fuel use and greenhouse gas emissions will be required. For a start, the cuts agreed under Kyoto are extremely modest—just 5 percent, and only apply to the world's wealthiest nations. To really deal with global warming, it is estimated that these countries will need to cut their emissions by more than 60 percent. Meantime, there's also the rest of the world to consider. Kyoto carries no goals for these nations at all. Although most developing countries have very low carbon dioxide emissions, they are rising fast, as the developing world tries to play catch-up on the economic front. Persuading these countries to take on emissions targets will not be easy. After all, they did not cause the problem; one might ask, Why should they not be allowed to develop economically by using fossil fuels as have the United States, Europe and Japan? Oil, gas and coal have a long history as the largest source of energy, and have fuelled the world's richest economies for many decades. Why should developing countries struggle with newer technologies like, say, wind or solar power, when coal- or gas-fired power stations offer a cheaper, easier alternative that's already been tried and tested in the industrialized world?

In fact, the traditional view that it is too expensive and damaging to the economy to shift away from fossil fuels is slowly starting to unravel. Economists are increasingly acknowledging the financial benefits of reducing reliance on fossil fuels, particularly given the recent trend toward high oil prices. The price of alternative forms of energy is coming down. And huge cost savings are possible for governments and big business that cut their emissions. According to a recent report by The Climate Group, a consulting firm, some industrialized countries have made significant amounts of money from cutting carbon dioxide emissions. "This debunks the myth that it always costs you money to cut carbon dioxide emissions. . . . [R]educing greenhouse gas emissions not only does not have to cost the earth, but can result in real value creation," said spokesperson Steve Howard in late 2004. According to the report, Britain's Action Energy Program saved the country more than one billion dollars from cutting emissions, while Germany's support for renewable energy has resulted in nearly half a million new jobs. Major multinationals, too, have saved billions of dollars. With so many industrialized countries taking on commitments under Kyoto, and growing evidence that it is not harming them economically, developing countries may ultimately come around to the idea that it is time to look beyond the modest start made at Kyoto and develop further international commitments for combating climate change.

REGIONAL AND NATIONAL RESPONSES

If international action on climate change has made limited progress so far, it has at least set the global community heading down the right path and, for the most part, in the same general direction. The climate change convention and Kyoto Protocol have also focused attention on global warming at a regional and national level, too. The Convention in particular has helped secure financial support from aid agencies such as the Global Environment Facility, a source of funding for climate change projects in the Third World set up by the UN and World Bank in 1991. To date, the Global Environment Facility has provided close to $5 billion to support literally hundreds of environmental projects in dozens of countries, with much of it going toward climate change activities such as small-scale solar power projects to bring electricity to rural parts of Africa, or schemes to make power stations less polluting.

The convention has also had an impact on many governments, raising the profile of global warming and encouraging regional cooperation and considerable action at the domestic level. Almost every nation on earth has changed its local laws and introduced new initiatives designed to help control emissions or to adapt to the effects of climate change. For instance, China has undertaken significant reforms aimed at encouraging energy efficiency and developing wind and solar technologies; it even plans on helping train as many as 10,000 experts from Africa and other parts of the Third World in applying solar energy technologies, thus sharing its expertise. The Netherlands is planning to slash its emissions by a massive 80 percent in the long term, while the UK, one of the world's economic heavyweights, has taken on targets that are almost as ambitious. In January 2005, the European Union introduced a regionwide emissions trading scheme that uses the same market-based approaches adopted by the Kyoto Protocol. The European scheme is expected to create a market for trading in the "right" to emit greenhouse gases valued at up to $15 billion annually. Meanwhile, from Mexico to Malawi, Brazil to Bangladesh, governments have been developing and introducing policies to respond to the climate change problem, from plans to control fossil fuel use to steps to adapt to the impacts global warming has already had. Even in the much-maligned United States, the Bush administration released a comprehensive policy document in 2002 outlining a wide variety of measures, from tax incentives to funding for developing renewable power from hydrogen.

The Kyoto Protocol has also inspired many countries to take further action, especially those wealthier nations that have pledged to cut their emissions. In particular, many nations are starting to experiment with the "flexible mechanisms" included in the treaty—the clean development mechanism, joint implementation and emissions trading.

LOCAL RESPONSES

National governments are not the only groups active on climate change. At both a local and national level, environment and conservation groups, businesses, academics, scientists, local authorities, unions, farmers and literally millions of individual citizens have been trying to make a difference in ways as varied as planting trees, conducting ground-breaking new research, funding renewable technology ideas, separating out trash that can be recycled, buying environmentally friendly products, or lobbying their elected officials. The media has also played an important role—although perhaps less so in the United States than elsewhere, as the next chapter will reveal. But whether it's at the local, state, national, regional or international level, many people are already actively seeking to play their part.

IS IT ENOUGH?

Clearly, a start has been made in combating climate change. Countless people around the world are aware of the problem. International treaties have been signed. National laws have been developed. Local action is taking place.

But is it really enough? The evidence says no. The experts are convinced that we need to contain our fossil fuel use and slash our emissions of carbon dioxide significantly if we are to prevent climate change from causing major damage to the planet's health, not to mention our own health and that of our economy. But even with the efforts outlined so far, global energy consumption is set almost to double in the first 30 years of this century. This wouldn't be a problem if the increase was going to come from environmentally friendly forms of energy such as wind or solar. It isn't. In spite of the dire warnings about what more fossil fuel use will do to our climate, on current trends, 90 percent of the growth in demand for energy is likely to be met by gas, oil and coal. According to the International Energy Agency, oil is more in demand than ever, and supplies are expected to jump from 75 to 120 million barrels a day by 2030. The impact on our emissions of greenhouse gases could be catastrophic.

The increasing demand for fossil fuels is not the only evidence that we are failing in our efforts to rein in the problem of global warming. In 2004, new measurements of the concentrations of carbon dioxide in our atmosphere broke all previous records, heightening fears that climate change may be spiraling out of control. The latest statistics continue a trend of sharp rises in recent years, with current carbon dioxide levels rising to 379 parts per million. Not surprisingly, projections of future climate change and its effects continue to become increasingly pessimistic; a spate of studies in 2004 pointed to a raft of deadly consequences, including an increase in the number of killer heat waves across Europe and North America of the type that cost tens of thousands of lives in France and elsewhere in 2003. Other research carried warnings of massive sea-level rise and floods that could engulf places as far apart as New Orleans, New York, London and the coasts of Bangladesh. Another new study by Professor Chris Thomas of the University of Leeds in the UK found that changes to our climate may be so extreme they could drive over one million species into extinction by 2050 (see chapter three for more).

A series of climate-related disasters in 2004 and early 2005 seemed only to hammer home these fears, lending further weight to the avalanche of new research arguing for more urgent action. Although not every extreme weather event can be attributed to climate change, the sudden rash of disasters around the world heightened fears that such events are on the rise.

With such a weight of evidence that the situation is deteriorating rapidly, it is clear that more needs to be done—a lot more.

CHAPTER SIX

WHAT GOVERNMENT AND BIG BUSINESS SHOULD BE DOING— AND WHY SOME VESTED INTERESTS DON'T WANT IT TO HAPPEN

The threat of climate change has been on the radar screen for a considerable length of time. As the previous chapter showed, governments, lobbyists, green groups and the public have been involved in various initiatives to start dealing with the problem. From international treaties such as the UN Climate Change Convention and the Kyoto Protocol to curbside recycling schemes operating on streets and towns throughout North America, Europe and other parts of the world, many people have been actively trying to find solutions to the ever-growing challenge.

But is it enough? Sadly, the answer is no. Much more needs to happen. So what should governments and big business be doing to help? And why haven't they acted more decisively when the magnitude of the problem is already so clear?

WHAT GOVERNMENT AND BIG BUSINESS SHOULD BE DOING

When it comes to government action, there is a lot more that needs to happen. Governments around the world have barely begun to scratch the surface of the problem. Embarrassingly for the people of the United States, its government's record is worse than most. The Bush administration and Congress have been negligent at best. For a start, they need to make a genuine commitment to international cooperation on this issue, to finding multilateral solutions. No one country can deal with a global problem of this magnitude by itself—not even a superpower like the United States.

Revisiting Kyoto?

"You're either with us or against us," George Bush announced in late 2001 shortly after launching the global war against terrorism. The same is true of global warming. As the world's biggest polluter, the United States needs to return to the international negotiating table and discuss how it can make a meaningful commitment to solving the problem. If the U.S. government does not engage more and become part of the global solution, it is effectively making America and its people a part of the problem—not something any U.S. citizen would want knowing the disastrous implications for their own health and safety that failure to address this problem might bring.

Ideally, the U.S. government should rejoin the fold and sign up to the Kyoto Protocol. After all, the Protocol is now an internationally recognized treaty in spite of the Bush administration's initial skepticism. And in spite of the doomsayers, many experts believe it will create all sorts of economic opportunities as well as the expected costs. American businesses should be able to exploit the incentives offered by the Protocol to profit from the development and distribution of new technologies and other forms of trade and international cooperation. While some economists point to various short-term costs in cutting emissions, there would also be some short-term gains. For instance, taking action to cut emissions would bring many financial benefits to companies both large and small. Making cars, homes, factories and offices more energy efficient would help restrain our burgeoning use of fossil fuels, too—which in turn would make America less reliant on imported oil from the Middle East and elsewhere. For businesses, cutting emissions by energy conservation initiatives is an easy way to cut costs and improve a company's bottom line. Combating climate change could create a lot of new jobs, too. Support for new industries such as those dealing with renewable energies like solar and wind might also help breathe fresh life into the economy. This has certainly been the case in Germany, which has witnessed the creation of half a million jobs as a result of the government's support for energy efficiency and renewable energy programs.

As well as the short-term gains, it is worth considering the long-term costs of *not* dealing with the problem now. Insurance losses rising to hundreds of billions of dollars a year, a jump in climate-related illnesses that could lead to a spike in health care costs, and massive financial losses caused by an increasing number of extreme weather events, such as heavy floods or heat waves—all are possible if we ignore the problem or fail to take it seriously enough.

At this stage, the chances of the United States ratifying the Kyoto Protocol appear slim. But, it is not impossible that the United States could become more open to Kyoto, or something similar, at some stage in the future. In 2003, the Senate considered a bipartisan bill that would have imposed Kyoto-style limits on greenhouse gas emissions. The bill was introduced by Senators John McCain and Joe Lieberman—one a Republican, the other a Democrat. Although the bill was voted down, it received more support than many had expected. In 2004, the bill was introduced into the House of Representatives. While it was not voted on, it again secured bipartisan support. The legislation was reintroduced into both houses of Congress in early 2005, suggesting that many politicians are now beginning to recognize the seriousness of the problem.

A report from the U.S. government's Climate Change Science Program released in the fall of 2004 signaled a possible shift in the White House, too. The report seemed to endorse the need for action when it acknowledged that global warming is indeed resulting from human activities. In the past, President Bush and his officials had downplayed the links between greenhouse gas emissions and global warming.

"The Bush administration's long overdue admission, in a new report to Congress, that global warming both exists and poses risks to people and the environment is a welcome step in the right direction," said conservation group WWF's American climate change director Katherine Silverthorne when the new report was released. "But belated recognition of a long-established scientific consensus on human-caused warming only helps if it leads to solutions," she added.

A key part of the solution is for the United States to agree to join other countries in taking on emissions targets. The world would welcome America taking this kind of leadership role. Some experts have even discussed whether or not a new deal could be struck to replace or supplement Kyoto. Perhaps the United States could negotiate with the European Union, China and a few other major polluters that together are responsible for most of the world's carbon emissions. While this is certainly a possibility, some fear that an alliance of just a handful of countries—no matter how powerful—would weaken the multilateral "one for all and all for one" approach to the problem by excluding countless countries from Africa, Latin America and elsewhere.

Whatever happens, though, the United States must be part of the international solution to global warming. Kyoto is probably the best way forward, but in the longer term new treaties will be required that build on our first modest steps. A future deal will need to include stronger commitments from a larger group of countries. Negotiating such commitments will not be easy, though. Persuading developing nations like China, India and Brazil to limit their future emissions could be a hard sell. In their view, global warming is a problem that was caused by the wealthiest countries as they followed a path to increasing affluence during the nineteenth and twentieth centuries. China or India could easily question why they should not be able to do the same. After all, their people deserve to live in material comfort and prosperity, too, don't they? And although emissions are rising in the Third World, these countries could point out that industrialized states still produce far more emissions on a per capita basis, averaging the equivalent of around 13 tons of carbon dioxide per person every year. Some, such as the United States, Canada and Australia, produce in excess of 20 tons per person. By comparison, China could rightly observe that it produces little more than 3 tons per person, while parts of Africa produce less than 1.

While major developing countries like China and India might be skeptical at first, persuading them to take on emissions targets like the ones adopted by most industrialized countries under the Kyoto treaty is essential in the long run. By first agreeing to targets of its own, the United States could help lead the way in making this happen. Countries like China are already wrestling with the question of how they can continue to develop and bring their people out of poverty without ruining the environment. New economic data suggest that cutting fossil fuel use and employing alternative energy sources is fast becoming a cost-competitive option. China and others know, too, that in the long run they will suffer badly if climate change is allowed to get out of hand—something that will surely happen if they do not keep their emissions under control. A visionary U.S. administration could well make all the difference when it comes to negotiating just such a new agreement with China and other developing countries.

The State of the Nation

Cooperating internationally is just the start. Within the United States, much more needs to happen. The Bush administration has simply not taken its responsibilities seriously. It has downplayed the risks, refused to limit U.S. emissions and tried to weaken some environmental legislation, including the prohibition on oil exploration in protected areas. It has also given the green light to the construction of upward of 1,000 new coal-fired power plants—at a time when it should be discouraging, not promoting, fossil fuel use. Even some of its pro-environment measures are suspect. For instance, plans to give a priority to improving "energy intensity" are not as impressive once you read the fine print. Energy intensity is a way of measuring the amount of energy required for each dollar earned by the economy. Improved energy intensity means that less energy is required for each dollar generated. The idea is that less oil, coal and gas can be used to create the same amount of energy and, ultimately, the same (or even more) wealth. While this is certainly a good thing, it is not the same as actually cutting emissions. All the government's plan actually means is that energy use will not grow quite as fast as the economy. But as the economy grows pretty much every year, energy use is still likely to grow, too. That's hardly as impressive as other countries' commitments to actually *cut* their emissions, especially when some of those countries, such as the United Kingdom, Ireland and New Zealand, often enjoy economic growth rates that are similar to those of the United States. Britain's economy grew by 36 percent from 1990 to 2002, while its greenhouse gas emissions actually declined by 15 percent during the same period. It is also worth bearing in mind that energy intensity in the U.S. has been improving in recent years anyway, so the Bush administration's plan is hardly groundbreaking.

Another much-feted federal policy is the support the government is providing for the development of new technologies that would allow the generation of power from hydrogen. The U.S. government plans to spend in excess of one billion dollars researching this possibility. In theory, this is a good idea, as hydrogen may ultimately provide a perfect source of abundant, cheap and environmentally friendly energy. But while its hydrogen plan certainly deserves praise, the government has been criticized, too, for being too optimistic. For a start, hydrogen research is a complex science that is unlikely to produce any meaningful benefits for decades to come. While the government clearly hopes it could prove to be a "silver bullet solution" that could start weaning the country off its dependence on foreign oil in the next 10–15 years, many remain skeptical. A new report from the National Academy of Sciences found that the complex scientific, technical and economic challenges faced in making hydrogen power affordable mean it will probably not replace oil and other fossil fuels for many decades to come. Instead, the report suggested a strategy focusing more on energy efficiency and other alternative energy sources. Some environmental groups have also criticized the administration's focus on hydrogen for being too speculative. They worry that it puts too many of the administration's eggs in one basket. What happens if the hydrogen research doesn't pay off, or happens too slowly to prevent serious climate change from happening?

Another question mark can be placed over the federal position on nuclear power. The government has considered an increase in nuclear power as one option in the fight against climate change. While it is true that nuclear energy avoids the use of fossil fuels, it raises the specter of other environmental problems, including the disposal of nuclear waste, the costs of decommissioning old plants and the risks of potentially dangerous nuclear accidents like those at the Chernobyl and Three Mile Island plants. To be fair, the United States is not the only country entertaining the nuclear option—Britain has also been debating increasing its reliance on nuclear power recently, while the French have long depended on it as their major source of electricity. Even some respected environmentalists favor its use. However, there are clearly some risks associated with nuclear energy that do not exist for other options such as wind or solar power. Investing just a fraction of the amount previously devoted to nuclear into these other options would help make them cost effective.

The policies listed above are not the only ones introduced in recent years by the federal government. A broad range of strategies are being pursued, including programs relating to electricity, transportation, industry, agriculture, forestry and residential and commercial buildings. Various voluntary partnerships with the private sector have been developed, from promoting energy-efficient offices to supporting recycling in the workplace. In addition, tax incentives to encourage energy efficiency and renewable forms of energy have been introduced. But it is not enough. At a national level, the government needs to be devoting considerably more funding and attention to the problem, reviewing its tax policies as they relate to fossil fuels and their alternatives, ending subsidies that encourage coal and oil and raising support for renewable energies such as wind and solar power.

Perhaps the federal government's relative neglect of climate change explains why some state governments have been so proactive on the issue. Many states seem to have been eager to fill the gap left by Capitol Hill in terms of providing political leadership on the problem. Some, such as Massachusetts and California, are even introducing emissions targets for certain industries. Meanwhile, in 2004, New York's attorney general joined those from seven other states in suing the country's biggest utilities for causing global warming. The lawsuit carried echoes of earlier cases against the powerful tobacco industry, in that it makes the case that these companies are responsible for a problem that is causing untold harm to Americans' health and well-being.

This could well be just the start as far as litigation is concerned. By early 2005, 10 legal cases had been announced around the world, according to conservation group Friends of the Earth. However, the group warned that this could be just the tip of the iceberg. "We will see a much longer queue of affected communities using the courts for compensation and justice unless we see deep cuts in greenhouse gas emissions," predicted Friends of the Earth spokesperson Catherine Pearce. As far as the United States is concerned, the policies preferred at the state level are likely to vary. However, the willingness of an increasing number of elected officials to promote policies targeting global warming is encouraging. It needs to be supported and maintained.

The State of Business

Surprisingly, some businesses have been far more progressive than the White House or Congress when it comes to climate change. While some powerful multinationals continue to view global warming as a threat to their business, others certainly do not. Even some in the oil industry are taking a pro-active approach. Companies such as BP and Shell have taken an increasingly forward-looking perspective on the subject, accepting that climate change is happening and positioning themselves increasingly as "energy" companies involved not just in fossil fuels like oil and gas, but also in the development of solar power and other more environmentally friendly forms of energy. In 1999, both left the Global Climate Coalition, a large business lobby group that was skeptical about climate change. Other major companies, like DuPont, have introduced hugely successful greenhouse gas emissions reductions schemes of their own, cutting their emissions (and their energy costs) significantly. Meanwhile, Toyota and Honda are leading the way in the auto industry with new, more environmentally friendly "hybrid" cars—closely followed by General Motors, Ford, DaimlerChrysler and the rest (see chapter seven for more on this).

Increasingly, then, big business is taking the climate change threat seriously. The risks and uncertainties that climate change could bring worry them. The private sector wants a business climate that is secure and predictable. Global warming threatens this. In the future, government and big business will need to cooperate even more, though, if the problem is to be dealt with. What has been achieved so far represents a good start, but nothing more.

WHY SOME VESTED INTERESTS WANT TO HIDE THE TRUTH

While some in the business world have recognized that climate change is happening, others have been more reluctant to accept it. In particular, businesses that could be affected by a shift away from oil, coal and gas seem to feel particularly vulnerable. Many of these companies are extremely powerful. According to their critics, some of them are trying to stifle debate on the issue and keep the truth about global warming from the public.

"Since the early 1990s, the fossil fuel lobby has mounted an extremely effective campaign of deception and disinformation designed to persuade policymakers, the press, and the public that the issue of climate change is stuck in scientific uncertainty," claimed veteran reporter Ross Gelbspan in 2004. Gelbspan accused the top executives of oil and coal industries of using "hired guns" to pose as greenhouse skeptics. "Most are laughingstocks in the scientific community," he concluded.

Gelbspan is not alone. Many of the world's experts on climate change have expressed concerns that a small group of vocal publicity seekers are hijacking the debate, and are misleading the public, the politicians and the media about what is really going on. While the science was far from certain 15 or 20 years ago, it is now. There is a consensus among mainstream scientists that climate change is happening, and must be taken seriously. The noisy handful of so-called experts who deny global warming are now about as credible as people who still think the Earth is flat or smoking won't damage your health. In an article published in late 2003, climate experts George Marshall and Mark Lynas identified and assessed the work of the few remaining climate skeptics they felt were muddying the waters. These included Bjorn Lomborg, a Danish statistician who authored *The Skeptical Environmentalist,* a work that they (and others) accuse of lacking academic rigor and objectivity. Other leading skeptics include astronomers Willie Soon and Sallie Baliunas, whose most recent report was dismissed by a number of climate experts. Marshall and Lynas point out that only one of the remaining skeptics is actually a legitimate climate scientist. Most also have links to right-wing think tanks or the oil industry.

While these skeptics have been discredited within the climate change community, however, their voices are still being heard everywhere else, particularly in the United States. The Bush administration's close links to the oil industry mean these questionable messages are still being heard at the highest political levels. A number of senior Bush administration officials are closely linked to the fossil fuel sector—Vice President Dick Cheney was head of Halliburton, a large oil services company, while Condoleezza Rice was once on the board of directors at Chevron. It's hardly surprising, then, that the oil industry can persuade those in the White House to lend a sympathetic ear to their concerns.

Some of the messages big business has been sending to our leading politicians are blunt, to say the least. In 2002, the Competitive Enterprise Institute referred to global warming as "the least important global environmental issue," and warned U.S. negotiators attending a major international summit to "keep it off the table and out of the spotlight." The Institute receives funding from ExxonMobil and various other multinational corporations.

Industry lobbyists even played a major role in developing the Bush administration's national energy strategy, according to experts from the Natural Resources Defense Council. The Council has released official documents it says show that lobbyists actually *wrote* a lot of the administration's energy policy themselves. According to the Council, "the administration sought the advice of polluting corporations early and often and then incorporated their recommendations into its policy, sometimes verbatim."

Oil industry lobbying goes beyond the Bush administration. A recent study showed that the U.S. oil and gas industry spent nearly half-a-billion dollars lobbying many of the politicians on Capitol Hill in recent years. The study revealed that some leading politicians had received significant industry support for their campaigns. The study, which was conducted by a bipartisan not-for-profit group, the Center for Public Integrity, sparked further accusations from anti-Bush campaigners that the oil industry had gained excessive influence over the federal government: "No industry in the history of the Republic has had former company executives sitting in the White House as President and Vice President, along with other very senior leadership positions," said Charles Lewis, the Center's director.

U.S.-based oil lobbyists are not shy about applying their influence internationally, either. In 2002, Robert Watson, a British-born

American who had advised the Clinton administration on climate change for many years, suddenly was ousted as chair of the Intergovernmental Panel on Climate Change—the world's most widely respected scientific body on global warming. According to insiders, Watson fell afoul of George Bush's administration not because of his association with Clinton, but because of his increasingly strident warnings to international audiences about the need to take climate change seriously. These warnings were based on comprehensive and compelling science endorsed by the world's most respected climate experts. In spite of this, Watson was replaced by a leading Indian expert, Rajendra Pachauri, who continues to lead the IPCC to this day. The change was greeted enthusiastically by some in the Third World, who were happy that such a prestigious international agency was being run by an expert from a developing country. But Republicans were delighted, too, as were many oil industry lobbyists—who were reportedly angry at Watson for taking such a firm line on the need for action, and who apparently played a major role behind the scenes in bringing about his downfall.

The impact of vested interests that oppose the climate change cause has been felt beyond just political circles. For a start, the U.S. media still gives ample coverage to the climate skeptics, frequently suggesting that the science of climate change remains disputed. It does not. Mainstream science is convinced that climate change is happening. No credible scientist disputes this. The rest of the world's media appears to have realized this already. According to Gelbspan, no other country's media, with the possible exception of Russia, still questions whether global warming is happening. They accept it, and have now all moved on to debating what should be done about it. Gelbspan believes the U.S. media has been targeted by a heavy campaign from big business lobbyists who complain strongly if television networks or other media give too much attention to climate change—particularly if they raise the possible connections between some freak weather event and global warming.

"The lobbyists . . . argue that you can't attribute any one extreme event to climate change—just as you cannot attribute any one case of lung cancer to smoking. But that is off point. The scientific community is unambiguous in its finding that the first and most visible manifestation of the planet's warming is an increase in violent weather extremes," says Gelbspan.

TAKING CONTROL

If the media is confused, it should hardly come as a great surprise that the public is, too—a suspicion that the surveys confirm. Frankly, Americans have been badly shortchanged when it comes to the truth about climate change and its likely effects. They deserve better. Better from their politicians, better from the media, better even from the big companies whose shares they own and whose products and services they buy every day. Perhaps, secretly, we don't really want to know about climate change? Perhaps it is easier to believe the flimsy evidence offered up by the handful of discredited experts rather than face the truth that there is an impending crisis. Perhaps it is easier to be in denial, to believe that the climate change science is still flaky, and that it is those warning us of the problem, and not the skeptics, who are in the minority.

Whether we're in denial or not, it is time for us to face up to the facts. Global warming is happening and it is a big problem. What's more, it is high time for us to take matters into our own hands, take control, and do something about it.

Chapter Seven

What Can I Do?

Global warming is probably the greatest threat facing humanity in the twenty-first century. As this book has already demonstrated, it could make our fears about terrorism or instability in the Middle East seem like small potatoes. Climate change threatens us with killer heat waves, wildfires, droughts, famines, floods, storms, new diseases and financial disaster. It is a blight that could even lead countries to war over the world's diminishing resources. It is putting at risk our health, our economy, our families, our future, our way of life.

If the problem seems daunting, it is. But it is not unstoppable. Like the best Hollywood action film, global warming presents us with the threat of impending disaster. Only this time, it is you who must play the heroic figure that rescues the planet from destruction. Although the crisis is almost upon us, you can still save the day. The latest predictions for the United States, for instance, show that what happens next depends almost entirely on us. Do nothing, continue just as we have been doing, and temperatures could leap by a massive 16°F across parts of North America. The result will be a disaster of biblical proportions. But act now and, just like Indiana Jones or Spiderman, you can still snatch victory from the jaws of defeat. Act now and you can help keep a lid on the problem. Act now and you could thwart the threat of a 16°F boil-over, and instead restrict the mercury to a modest rise of just 2°F over the coming century.

So, you get to be the hero. And the good news is it won't even be that hard. Just a few straightforward steps and a few minutes of your time will help not only the planet, but also your family, your health, even your finances. Most Americans could easily save hundreds or even thousands of dollars every year just by taking a few basic measures. First, though, it's worth considering your power as a voter, and the influence you can have in making politicians take action.

VOTER POWER!

As the previous chapter showed, our elected officials should be doing a lot more to deal with the problem. For a start, they should be encouraging the use of renewable energy sources such as wind and solar, promoting fuel-efficient cars and energy efficiency around the home, and supporting international treaties to address the problem globally. Taking this type of action now will certainly make things easier later on, and could create new jobs and business opportunities across the country.

Vote for the Greenest Candidate

Making politicians sit up and take notice is less difficult than it might appear. To start with, make sure you vote, every chance you get! Sure, you're just one person. But your influence is greater than you imagine. Consider how close the presidential vote was in 2000, for instance—just a few hundred votes in one key state decided who won and lost. And this is not the only example; statistically, many votes for congressmen, senators and other elected officials are often extremely close. Just taking the time to vote could help force your elected official to take the problem seriously—or could bring in a new person who will.

Exercising your democratic right to support a candidate that's taking global warming seriously is important. But how can you figure out who that candidate is? After all, everyone running for office is sure to *claim* the best credentials. Fortunately, help is at hand when it comes to deciding who you should believe. The League of Conservation Voters—or LCV—is a nonprofit group dedicated to promoting pro-environment policies in Congress and the White House. The League has been tracking the voting records of every politician on Capitol Hill since 1970, allowing voters to judge for themselves which officials can be trusted on environmental matters. The LCV has developed a great website providing scorecards for members of Congress and the administration so you can see through the rhetoric and hold your elected officials accountable for what they've done, not what they've promised to do. To learn more, visit www.lcv.org/scorecard/scorecardmain.cfm.

If you want to go a step further and research the records of individual senators or congressmen from your state, visit www.capwiz.com/lcv/dbq/vote_info. This site will let you put every major political figure in the country under the microscope. So whether you'd like to check up on Senator Hillary Clinton of New York, Kay Bailey Hutchison of Texas or Alabama's Richard Shelby, you'll find their individual voting records right here.

For those who would prefer an expert opinion on which officials are worth supporting, the LCV also provides its own list of endorsements and recommendations for candidates during every election year. While some critics believe the list is too liberal, the site makes it clear that it judges politicians purely on their environmental records, not on whether they are from the right or left of the political spectrum. And although the highest pro-environment scores do generally go to Democrats, the site does not shy away from endorsing Republicans, too, if their environmental records justify it. For instance, in 2004 the LCV strongly supported Republican Rob Simmons for reelection in Connecticut's second Congressional district, citing his excellent voting record on environmental issues, including his opposition to drilling in protected areas. To check the LCV's list of endorsements, visit www.lcv.org/Campaigns/CampaignsList.cfm?c=3. Meanwhile, if you're interested in finding the candidates with the *worst* records on the environment, try www.lcv.org/Campaigns/CampaignsList.cfm?c=1.

Lobby Your Elected Official

While exercising your right to vote can make a big difference, there is something else you can do that is even more important—lobby. As anyone who has worked in politics will tell you, most elected officials are extremely sensitive to the opinions of their constituents—after all, their future depends on it! This is especially true if a politician starts to receive many messages about the same issue. So if you can persuade friends and family to join the cause, your message will almost certainly be heard. And if it sounds like too much work, it isn't. Nowadays, many pro-environment organizations make it easy to send a message to your elected officials. Several allow you to make your feelings known through e-mail in less than 60 seconds. The LCV site has a section that lets you do this. It even has a section that helps you contact the media. Other excellent, user-friendly websites that will help you send a message to the bigwigs on Capitol Hill include those of the Natural Resources Defense Council (www.nrdcaction.org/action) and the National Wildlife Federation (www.nwf.org/action), which helps you make your views known on a range of green issues, including climate change. Both are well known and respected conservation groups. The National Wildlife Federation was founded in 1936 and boasts over four million members.

SAVE ENERGY, SAVE THE PLANET, AND SAVE $$$

So is voting and lobbying politicians to make *them* do something about the problem the only way *you* can make a difference? Far from it. The rest of this chapter sets out many simple steps you can take to fight global warming directly. Most are about conserving energy. That's because it is the energy we use—whether it's electricity generated from coal-fired power stations, or oil, or natural gas—that's causing global warming. Our modern world is pretty wasteful in its use of energy. And naturally, most energy companies *want* us to use more of the stuff, because that's how they make their money. But there are many easy ways to cut your energy use without it causing the least inconvenience or changing your way of life in any way. Even the smallest change will make a difference to our planet.

It will also make a difference to your wallet. Saving energy will save you money. Lots of money. The rest of this chapter deals with some simple cost-saving tips you can introduce in various aspects of your life—as a consumer when you're shopping, as a driver or commuter when you're using your car around town or traveling longer distances, and even in the comfort of your own home, backyard or garden. A comprehensive checklist of what you can do to save the planet (and your wallet) from climate change can be found at the end of the chapter.

Consumer Power!

If there is one thing that will make big business and the corporate set sit up and take notice, it's when you exercise your power as a consumer. There are many ways you can use your spending habits to combat global warming—and force retailers and manufacturers to take the problem seriously, too. Some of these steps will also save you money in the bargain.

Support Green Companies

Some companies are already taking climate change and other environmental matters seriously. Others, unfortunately, are not. There are now a number of organizations and agencies that attempt to monitor and evaluate companies' records on the environment. One of these, Co-op America, is a national nonprofit organization. Established in the early 1980s, it provides a lot of information online about how companies perform in regards to the environment, social responsibility and business ethics. For the consumer, Co-op America offers the Responsible Shopper service (www.responsibleshopper.com), which allows the public to compare the environmental friendliness of companies and even individual products. While the comparisons are somewhat open to debate, they do provide an informed opinion on how major companies stack up and are based on considerable research about each firm's record. So, if you want an expert's view on whether BP is better (or worse) than ChevronTexaco in how it runs its gas stations, or how the different department stores, banks or automakers compare, the Responsible Shopper site is a good place to start. Buying from companies that are taking environmental issues seriously sends a message that you recognize their efforts—and tells their competitors to shape up, too.

Another shopping tip is to buy products that have recyclable packaging. The recycling logo is easy to spot (see figure 7.1). If you have a choice of packaging (for instance, if you're buying a drink), glass should be your first choice, as it's the easiest to recycle. Aluminum is next, followed by paper and plastic. You could also try buying products that come from material that's already been recycled. This includes containers made of glass and aluminum, but only some paper and plastic (again, it should tell you on the packaging).

Invest in Green Companies

If you invest in the stock market—and nearly half of all adult Americans do—you can have an impact, too, by supporting companies that are socially and environmentally responsible. If you're investing in a company, you're helping to finance what it does. But what if the business actually has a bad environmental record, or a history of human rights abuses? You may not know it, but your investments could be supporting a company that is systematically damaging people and the planet. By taking a little time to check up on the companies you invest in, you can push them to be more socially and environmentally responsible.

You won't be alone, either. These days, many people are starting to pay greater attention to the ethics of the companies

Figure 7.1   This symbol, with three arrows bending to point toward the
next, indicates that the product's packaging can be recycled.

they invest in. An estimated 10 percent of all investments are now
labeled "socially responsible." This kind of economic activism
really works, too; some experts believe that people taking their
money out of South Africa in the 1970s and 1980s helped end
apartheid, while in recent years some companies have been prod-
ded into cleaning up their act on environmental issues, too. Investing in companies that care about social issues and the
environment also makes sound business sense. When you're
looking for a safe place to invest your money, you should be seeking a company that is thinking long-term about how it can maxi-
mize shareholder value. As this book has demonstrated, global
warming presents some huge threats and challenges to companies—and some opportunities, too. For a start, many countries,
including the United States, are introducing new laws and regu-
lations to respond to global warming. Then there are the huge insurance cost implications of climate change, including the
expected rise in weather-related disasters and damage. And that's
just the tip of the iceberg. What this means is that any business
that's still ignoring the threat of climate change is not positioning
itself to deal effectively with these challenges as they arise. How
can they possibly be sustainable or successful over the long term?
Studies already confirm this, showing that companies that score
well on environmental and social responsibility criteria often
outperform the stock market. A helpful introduction to responsible investing is available online at www.naturalchoice.net/
articles/sri.htm.

Mutual Funds

If you invest in mutual funds—which is the way most people invest in the stock market these days—an excellent source of free advice is the www.CookingYourNestEgg.org website. This site is run by Results for America, a nonprofit group based in Massachusetts that monitors companies' performance on climate change. The site will tell you if a particular company or mutual fund has a poor record in responding to the problem. The site notes that companies that drag their heals on climate change could ultimately see their share price drop due to a consumer backlash or because their lack of foresight means they fail to find cost savings, exploit new business opportunities or avoid the risks arising from global warming. The site, which was launched in September 2004, could help you avoid investing in companies with a poor track record on climate issues.

Another source of information on how companies are dealing with climate change is the Coalition for Environmentally Responsible Economies (CERES). Be warned, though—the CERES website is not for the faint-hearted, offering detailed advice for those who really want to immerse themselves in the issue of responsible investment. CERES has recently published a no-holds-barred report on how some of the world's largest companies are performing when it comes to global warming, questioning the record of some leading companies such as ExxonMobil, DaimlerChrysler and General Electric, while praising others (www.ceres.org/newsroom/press/ceresirrcrel.htm). A second report from CERES offers in-depth advice for the more serious investor to help them minimize their exposure to the financial risks of global warming while benefiting from the potential opportunities (www.ceres.org/newsroom/press/ig_release.htm).

Other organizations offering more general advice about socially and environmentally responsible mutual funds include the Social Investment Forum, the Social Funds Group and the Calvert Group and Domini investment funds.

When Less Is More

These days, we live in a very consumer-driven society. But how much of what we own do we really need? Take a moment to check your closet, attic, garage or basement. If they're crammed with things you don't need and never use, you're not alone. Our modern society is geared toward selling us as much as we can afford (and more), much of which we don't really need. The more we buy, the stronger the signal we send to manufacturers to keep burning fossil fuels by churning out new products, gadgets and gimmicks. So next time you're thinking of that new gizmo you saw advertised on the tv, ask yourself if you really need it after all. Resisting the urge will save you money and help protect the planet from climate change.

Reducing the amount of consumer goods you buy is probably the single best thing you can do for the environment. It comes first in the three-word mantra that in recent years has become well known to all environmentalists. This is the "3 Rs" . . . and no, it doesn't mean reading, writing and arithmetic. In eco-friendly parlance, the 3 Rs refer to "reducing, reusing and recycling" what we buy. Although you should try to practice all three, reducing our demand is actually the best of all—better even than recycling. That's because, unlike recycling, which is about finding a better way to deal with all the garbage we produce, reducing our demand for goods means we're actually reducing waste by cutting down on the amount of packaging and trash we produce in the first place.

Of course, you can't reduce your demand for everything. Some things you really *do* need. Food, toiletries, new shoes or school supplies for the kids—some items are absolutely essential. Even here, though, you can still save money while also helping the environment. For instance, when it comes to some foodstuffs or items for your kitchen or bathroom, bulk buying can help. Often it's cheaper, and it also usually results in less packaging. So the next time you're shopping for soap or toilet paper or canned food, consider the bulk buying option. Also, watch out for overstocking perishables. If you notice you're buying too much of something—whether it's bread, apples or whatever—and consistently end up throwing it away, it's worth asking whether you actually need it in the first place.

Second-Hand Goods Are Cool: Pass It On . . .

Of course, manufacturers are going to tell you it's only cool if it's new. After all, they want you to buy their shiny, pristine products. But second-hand—or pre-loved, if you prefer—is *in* these days. It is also good for the environment, because reusing items means we're expending less energy making new ones. So when you're spring cleaning, check out what items you don't need anymore. Perhaps you have a collection of vests you don't want; you decide you'll never use your old stereo again; or you find you've somehow ended up with three extra dinner sets. You might not want them, but someone else probably will.

Giving your old stuff away can give you a warm glow, and there are thousands of charity stores that would love to have them. Alternatively, you could try selling them online, or having a good old-fashioned yard sale. Yard sales can be a fun way to get rid of some of your old things while making a bit of cash at the same time. You might want to talk to your neighbors to see if they are interested in having a sale, too, as more people are likely to show up if it becomes a big event. You could advertise in your local paper and perhaps post signs around your neighborhood on the day of the sale. You could also post news of your sale on the Internet. For more advice about holding a yard sale (and to advertise your event for free), visit www.yardsalesearch.com.

Bag It!

By now, you're probably getting the message that reusing things is far better for the environment than getting something new. Remember the little shopping bag your Gran used to carry everywhere? She had the right idea. Unfortunately, times have changed. Every time you buy something these days, someone seems to want to give you a free plastic or paper bag to carry it in. But, do you really need them? In Germany, the government decided to ask people to start bringing their own bags, to cut down on all that plastic and paper being produced. Unfortunately, Americans still go through 100 *billion* grocery bags every year. These plastic and paper bags cause untold damage to our environment. Plastic bags take hundreds of years to decompose and are now causing huge problems both on land and at sea, reportedly killing hundreds of thousands of sea turtles, birds, and other species that get tangled in them, or that swallow them after mistaking them for food (turtles apparently confuse them with jellyfish, and choke to death on them).

Plastic bags are also bad for the economy. The reason for this is that producing plastic bags requires oil. A lot of oil. One estimate suggests that the United States alone needs 12 million barrels of oil to meet its yearly demand for plastic bags. Cutting back on our use of these bags would help reduce our reliance on expensive foreign oil—which would help not just in the fight against global warming, but also in raising our economic growth. The cost of producing all these plastic bags has been estimated at several billion dollars annually—costs that retailers ultimately pass on to you, the consumer. Meanwhile, the use of paper grocery bags (10 billion a year just in the United States) also puts an unnecessary burden on the environment and economy, causing 15 million additional trees to be felled every year.

So, next time you go shopping, ask yourself if you really need new bags. If you're buying a candy bar at your corner store, or just a few items in the supermarket, try bringing your own cloth or plastic bags. You can keep them in the trunk of your car. The Reusable Bags company sells a wide range of bags, and is also a treasure trove of information on the bag problem (http://reusablebags.com).

Bringing your own bag could even save you money. In November 2004, San Francisco city officials announced that they were looking at placing a tax on supermarket bags to reflect the true costs to the environment and the economy. If the tax happens, it could end up costing consumers 17 cents for every new bag they use. A similar tax has already been introduced successfully in Ireland.

Reuse It

As well as shopping bags, other reusable items you might want to try include rechargeable batteries rather the throw-away ones, or razors in which you replace just the cartridge and not the whole thing. You could also try refilling your plastic or glass bottle (see the section on "The Water Scam"); taking your own mug or cup when you visit your local coffee shop instead of using their plastic, foam or paper ones; and even using old-fashioned cloth napkins and diapers rather than the disposable ones. And if something's broken, it's worth finding out whether it can be repaired rather than thrown away. For more advice on reusing things, check out the Reuse Development Organization's handy website (www.redo.org).

Think Global, Buy Local

Coconuts from the Caribbean, kiwi from Chile, champagne from, well, Champagne (in France, not Illinois). You can buy produce from pretty much anywhere these days. It sure seems like a small world! Actually, though, it's not, and it takes a huge amount of effort and energy to transport all these exotic products to your local store. In the process, many tons of carbon dioxide are spewed into the atmosphere by all those ships, trains and trucks carrying these products to every corner of the globe. To help combat global warming, try buying more local products. For instance, locally grown food requires less fossil fuel–burning transportation, and helps your local economy, too. The food you buy will almost certainly be fresher, which means it's also better for you. If your town has a farmers' market, check it out. A farmers' market allows local growers to sell direct to consumers. In recent years they have grown in popularity, with their numbers almost doubling between 1994 and 2002. Prices at these markets are often as cheap (or cheaper) than what you'll find in your supermarket. And it's probably better for you, too, since the produce is locally grown, meaning it has had less distance to travel, and is consequently likely to be fresh. A comprehensive listing of farmers' markets in the United States has been posted online and is available from the Department of Agriculture, so you can locate the one nearest you. And with over 3,000 markets in the United States, there will almost certainly be one close to wherever you're living, whether it happens to be in Manhattan (where 21 markets are listed) or places as diverse as Mesilla, New Mexico, Meridian, Mississippi, or Miles City, Montana (www.ams.usda.gov/farmersmarkets).

Organic Food Makes You Hip (Not a Hippy)

Organic food is not just for hard-core greenies or hippies. If you're wanting to help combat global warming, then this type of produce is a good way to go. The reason for this is that organic food does not contain many of the pesticides, herbicides and other chemicals used on more conventional crops. These chemicals have to be manufactured and then transported to the farms that use them, all of which burns huge amounts of oil and other fossil fuels.

Organic foods could well be better for your health, too. For a start, some experts believe organic crops contain more vitamins, minerals and other essential nutrients than their more conventional competitors. Not surprisingly, producers and sellers of regular food have hit back at claims that their produce is inferior. While the jury is still out on the matter, what is certain is that organic foods do meet very high standards these days. In 2000, the U.S. Department of Agriculture introduced rigorous requirements for farmers wishing to label their food as organic, requiring that they be made without the use of most conventional pesticides or synthetically produced fertilizers. Organic meat and dairy products are now required to use no antibiotics or growth hormones. Also, organic food is prohibited from using irradiation, sewage sludge or genetic engineering—any of which can be applied on conventional foods.

These high standards seem to be appealing to an increasing number of shoppers, offering peace of mind that their families are no longer being exposed to those worrying pesticides and chemicals that are sprayed on regular crops. So, give organic food a try—it is certainly a healthier option when it comes to combating climate change, and it's probably better for you, too.

Veg Out!

Vegetables are good for you—we all know that. But what most people don't know is that they're also good for the environment. You don't have to believe that "meat is murder"—but it is certainly true that "meat is methane," which is just as bad when it comes to global warming. This is because cows and other livestock produce methane when they burp or pass gas. Methane is a major greenhouse gas, second only to carbon dioxide in the contribution it is making to global warming. The manure produced by livestock also sends a lot of methane into our atmosphere. Cows in particular produce a large amount of methane. This is a real problem, because Americans are big meat eaters. Each year, the average American consumes almost 250 pounds of meat—mostly beef, pork and poultry. That's the equivalent of 1,000 McDonald's quarter pounders—each! To feed our obsession, the United States has about 100 million cows, 60 million hogs and pigs, 8 million sheep and lambs and 450 million poultry—which is not only a staggering number in its own right, but also means the chickens have us heavily outnumbered. Not that we're the only ones—globally, the world has more than 1.1 billion cattle and almost as many sheep helping to feed our meat frenzy. The livestock reared to meet our insatiable appetite for animal flesh contributes one quarter of America's *total* methane gas emissions, making it a major cause of global warming. And our meat fixation has only increased over the years, with consumption per person rising by almost one third since the 1950s.

What's more, rearing livestock is inefficient. It is far easier for farmers (and nature) to produce plants than animals. The production of just one pound of beef requires seven pounds of grain and a staggering 2,500 gallons of water. By contrast, it takes just 25 gallons of water to produce a pound of grain. Perversely, though, most of our grain goes toward producing meat. Currently, a staggering three quarters of the U.S. grain crop is consumed by cows and other livestock. By contrast, producing the same amount of fruit, grains or vegetables takes just a tiny fraction of the energy and resources. Just a small reduction in our meat intake would free up enough land to cause a big jump in our production of grains and other food, and could help some of the 800 million people around the world currently suffering from hunger and malnutrition.

Consuming more vegetables and a little less meat is not just better for the environment—it is also kinder on your wallet. Reducing your beef intake by just one meal a week could cut your annual shopping bill by $100. More vegetables and less meat can be good for your health, too. Studies show that those who consume more fruit and vegetables are less likely to suffer from heart disease, high cholesterol, obesity, diabetes and certain types of cancer than those who eat more meat and less of the green stuff. That's not to say that meat is bad. It contains protein and various minerals and nutrients that can form part of a healthy diet. But like anything, it's something that shouldn't be done to excess. And right now, many Americans arguably eat too much of it.

Of course, this doesn't mean you should instantly throw away the steaks and sausages and turn vegetarian to save the planet. But eating one less meal a week with meat in it (and especially red meat) will do you, your family, your wallet and your planet some good. Even if you can't bear the thought of a single meal without some meat in it, you can still make a difference by replacing some of your red meat intake with fish or poultry—producing these foodstuffs contributes less to global warming than beef and other red meat.

The Water Scam

Imagine that you were offered two almost identical products—one cost a few bucks every single day, while the other was free and just as safe (or safer). Which would you choose? Which would most people choose? If you guessed the free option, you're wrong. An increasing number of Americans are falling for the expensive alternative. Many experts view it as the biggest marketing miracle in a decade.

The scam is bottled water. These days, Americans are literally drowning in the stuff, paying two or three bucks for every bottle. The irony is, you can get the same substance from your faucet for free—and it's probably better for you! Studies show that tap water is generally as safe, and sometimes safer, than bottled water. What's more, a lot of bottled water is actually sourced from tap water. Is it really worth paying for something you can get for free?

One of the reasons for the new fad is the taste. In some places, tap water just doesn't seem to taste so good. If that's the case where you live, or if you just want added security that your tap water's safe (although safety standards are very high these days), try using a filter. There are several kinds that work well and will give you the cleanest water possible for a fraction of the price of bottled water. Faucet filters are attached to your sink, while you can also get some great pitcher filters that you can store in your fridge (you fill up the top part of the pitcher with water, which is then filtered into the main section). Meanwhile, a portable filtered bottle is perfect for people on the go who want the cleanest water available (Brita makes a good one). Any of these options is infinitely cheaper than bottled water. It also helps reduce demand for the production and transportation of bottled water, which is an unnecessary waste of energy. Why import water all the way from France when you can get something that is cheaper (and quite possibly safer) right from your faucet?

The same goes for water coolers. They're expensive and use a lot of energy. If you can, go for a filter instead. If you must have a water cooler, check its energy efficiency (www.energystar.com) before you buy.

TRAVEL POWER!

So you now know how to exercise your power as a consumer and an investor in the fight against climate change. But this is not the only area of your life where you can make a personal difference. Another way to have an impact is through your travel habits. Even a few simple changes would do some good to the planet—not to mention your wallet.

Your Deadly Car

Each year, your car pumps about five or six *tons* of carbon dioxide out of its exhaust. That's around 11,000 pounds of the greenhouse stuff from just *one* vehicle—the same as your entire house produces. If that sounds like a lot, try multiplying it by 542 million—the total number of passenger vehicles in the world today. What's worse, Americans are making the problem more serious than it should be. With just one-twentieth of the world's population, the United States has one-quarter of its cars. It should be no surprise, then, to learn that America's vehicles produce over 30 percent of the country's carbon dioxide emissions, contributing excessively to the global warming problem. Our cars also produce carbon monoxide and a cocktail of other dangerous gases that can cause a variety of health problems, including respiratory illnesses and even cancer. And it's getting worse—in recent years, our cars, trucks and other forms of transport registered faster growth in their emissions than any other sector of the economy.

Improve Your Car's Fuel Efficiency

The good news, though, is that there are some simple steps you can take to help fix the problem. You don't have to abandon your car or change your lifestyle to make a difference. For a start, a regular tune-up will make your vehicle run more efficiently, saving on the amount of gas you use—which is surely no bad thing given the prices at the pumps these days. You can help keep your car in good condition by having a mechanic give it a simple tune-up once every few months, changing the oil and checking the air filters, drive belts, radiator and so on. If you're mechanically inclined, you can probably do it yourself. Keeping your car in good condition will increase its fuel efficiency, which means less frequent trips to fill up the tank, and less carbon dioxide, too. You should also check at least once a month that your tires are inflated properly, as this can also help improve fuel efficiency.

Another way to make your car cost less is to drive at a more consistent speed. Many of us like to accelerate quickly and brake hard, especially when we're driving in towns and cities. Next time you drive, try going at a steadier pace, accelerating a little more gently, and braking less rapidly. It probably won't add to your travel time, but it will definitely improve your car's fuel efficiency, by as much as one third. Plus, it's a more relaxing, stress-free way to drive.

Finally, check the trunk. If you've got heavy items in there that you don't need, your vehicle is being forced to carry unnecessary weight. Taking it out could help improve your fuel efficiency a little more. If you have a ski rack or roof rack that you don't use much, take it off, too—the wind drag it creates could be adding 5 percent to the cost of your vehicle's gas habit. For more tips on fuel efficiency, visit www.fueleconomy.gov/feg/drive.shtml.

Control Your Car

It's no surprise that Americans (and Germans, and Japanese and many other nationalities) love their cars. For a start, they're so easy to use, so convenient. Just jump inside, hit the gas, and you can be at the mall, the office, school or wherever you need to be in no time—as long as you don't get caught in traffic, of course. But there is a cost. Unfortunately, we're also ruining our environment, and our health, in the process.

Just using your car a little less can help. For instance, if you have a few errands to run, try combining them all in one car trip, rather than using the car several times. You could also consider walking or biking to your local shops, assuming they're not too far. And with more than half of us now overweight, walking and biking are great ways to stay fit, too. There are no gym membership fees, either.

Shopping online is another way to help, as it is almost always better than taking your car out to buy the same stuff. And if you're a telecommuter, congratulations! Working from home just one or two days a week cuts down on your car use significantly. Some studies show that it generally results in employees being happier and more efficient, too!

Taking the train, subway or bus can also help. It's better for the environment, and by letting someone else do the driving, you get to read or work, which is a far more efficient use of your time than sitting behind the wheel in some traffic jam. Carpooling is another option that's worth considering. It's cheaper and often quicker, especially if your local freeway has a car pool lane. Carpooling just twice a week could save you hundreds of dollars and cut your carbon emissions by a massive 1600 pounds per year. Some basic carpooling tips are available on www.commuterpage.com/tentips.htm. There are a number of websites that help connect people who want to carpool locally, including: www.carpoolworld.com and www.erideshare.com.

Depending on where you live, there may be other options for your commute to work that save you money as well as helping save the environment. The U.S. government recently announced an initiative to help businesses offer cash benefits and other incentives for people to travel to work in ways that are less harmful to the environment. The *Commuter Choice* scheme involves businesses and other organizations across the country. The initiative takes a flexible approach, recognizing that each company, location and workforce are different. For instance, one program might offer financial incentives for workers who carpool, while another might subsidize workers who use public transport. Ask if your company is a part of this. If it isn't, it might wish to join, as there are various tax benefits they (and you) could enjoy. Even if your company is not interested, it may still offer travel benefits to its employees. The *Commuter Choice* initiative also provides specific information on commuting options in every state and major city in the United States. For more information, visit www.commuterchoice.com.

Change Your Car

So you've reined in your gas-guzzling, planet-polluting passenger car and made it work more efficiently. Maybe you're even walking to the shops or taking public transport to work sometimes? If so, you're making a big contribution in the war against global warming. But if you are in the market for a new car, there is something even better you can do.

Does S.U.V.=U.N.S.A.F.E.?

A few years back, sport utility vehicles suddenly became all the rage. In the 1990s and early 2000s, SUVs quickly grabbed the lion's share of the passenger vehicle market, surging from just 7 percent of all vehicle sales in 1990, to 24 percent in 2002—more than any other single vehicle category. Surveys suggested that people liked the bigger size of SUVs compared to regular passenger vehicles, as well as their greater height from the road surface. Both factors made them feel safer. Unfortunately, that feeling of safety could well be an illusion. In recent years, some experts have been warning that SUVs are a major menace on our roads that we could well do without. In 2003, National Highway Traffic Safety Administration chief Jeffrey Runge came out swinging on SUV safety. In particular, he raised fears about the risks of rollover accidents, as well as the dangers SUVs pose to smaller vehicles. While the auto industry has strongly defended its most popular product, it has acknowledged that some safety fears, such as the much higher chances of an SUV rolling over in a crash compared with other cars, may have some foundation. Figures released in the United States in 2004 showed that those driving or riding in an SUV were almost 11 percent more likely to die in an accident than people in passenger cars.

As well as the risks to those actually in an SUV, the large size of these vehicles makes them a risk to others, too. According to one study by the U.S. National Highway Traffic Safety Administration, SUVs are twice as likely to cause a fatality if they hit a regular passenger car than if two smaller cars collide. While the industry has defended SUVs and pledged to improve their safety record, the jury still appears to be out on how successful it has been. The lesson from all of this is that your family and friends may actually be safer if they drive a regular car.

They will certainly be better off. SUVs are horrific gas guzzlers, averaging a paltry 15 miles to the gallon, compared to around 25 miles per gallon for a standard passenger car. Every year, without fail, large SUVs dominate the list of vehicles that are the most costly to run and have the worst environmental effects. It adds up to a lot more dollars at the pump, and a lot more carbon dioxide in our atmosphere.

Some people might think SUVs are fashionable—after all, there are now more than 22 million of them on our roads. But how cool can something so inefficient, expensive to run and potentially dangerous really be?

The message that SUVs aren't so cool after all may finally be getting through. After their surge of popularity in the 1990s, SUV sales showed signs of losing their upward momentum in the first half of 2004, with vehicles remaining longer on dealer lots, and models such as the Ford Explorer and Ford Expedition actually showing a dip in popularity. While it is too soon to conclude whether this marks the start of a long-term trend, some experts have speculated that SUVs may no longer be seen by some as being as cool or fashionable as they were several years ago.

Another phenomenon that took off during the 1990s was the minivan. Again, these are gas guzzlers, although they can make sense if you have a big family. If there are less than five of you usually in the vehicle at any one time, though, a regular passenger car is a far more cost-effective option. To find a list of the most fuel-efficient cars, visit www.fueleconomy.gov or www.greenercars.com/bestof.html.

The Hype about Hybrids

At the very least, then, you should make your next vehicle something that's fuel-efficient and guzzles less gas. But if you want to go a step further, you should consider a car that uses cutting-edge technology to cut down on the use of "dirty" fuels such as gas or diesel. An increasingly fashionable option is the hybrid car. Running on a mix of regular gas and electricity, hybrid vehicles are just as easy to operate as other cars, because the electricity is produced while your car drives—it doesn't need to be plugged in, ever. You just drive it and fill up the tank with gas, as usual. They are just as powerful, fast and convenient as any other car, too. They even look like other cars.

The only difference comes at the pump. Because hybrids run partly on electricity, they use a lot less gas. Your hybrid will cost you about half as much to run as a regular car—with even greater savings if you're used to driving a bigger vehicle such as an SUV. Some hybrids get more than 50 miles to the gallon. The reason for this is that an electric motor assists the regular internal combustion engine. The electric motor gets its energy simply from the momentum generated whenever your car is running—which means you never need to plug it in or worry about charging it at all. But this new technology means huge cost savings when you're filling the tank. Some view the hybrid as the biggest breakthrough in vehicle technology in half a century. While their purchase price is a little higher, you will save literally thousands of dollars on gasoline during the car's lifetime, while cutting your carbon dioxide emissions in half. There are also tax deductions possible on some models, but you should get in quick, as these are likely to be phased out by 2007 (www.fueleconomy.gov/feg/tax_hybrid.shtml).

Their convenience and amazing gas mileage are making these new vehicles the hottest thing in the auto world in years. If SUVs were the new kids on the block in the 1990s, then hybrids are shaping up to be the fashion item of the future. Already, Hollywood celebrities such as Cameron Diaz, Tom Hanks, Meryl Streep, Sting, Tim Robbins, Jon Stewart and Leonardo DiCaprio have reportedly flocked to join the growing trend toward hybrids. And although the total number of sales is still small compared to more conventional vehicles, they're rising fast. Overall, sales rose 26 percent in 2003 compared to the previous year, and doubled in 2004, to around 80,000 in the United States alone. By 2008, some experts believe half a million will be leaving showrooms each year.

The first three hybrid cars to make an impact in the United States have been the Toyota Prius, the Honda Civic Hybrid and the smaller, hyperefficient Honda Insight. Although some felt hybrids would not catch on when they first appeared on the market in 2000, both Honda and Toyota are now reaping the rewards of being the first off the grid. In late 2004, demand for the Prius was growing so fast that Toyota was struggling to keep up with demand and was increasing production. Other auto manufacturers are joining the race to meet consumer demand, too. Affordable hybrid versions of several sedans, hatchbacks, SUVs and pickups went on sale in late 2004 and early 2005, including the Ford Escape, Honda Accord, Lexus RX 400, Chevy Silverado and GMC Sierra. Numerous other hybrid models are coming on-stream from the middle of 2005 onward, with as many as 30 hybrid models likely to be available by 2009. For the latest news on hybrid vehicles, visit www.fueleconomy.gov/feg/hybrid_news.shtml.

Other Options

If for some reason you don't like the idea of a hybrid, there are other alternatives, including gas-powered or electric vehicles. While these are not yet as convenient or easy to use as hybrids, they can also save you a lot of money. For more information, visit www.fueleconomy.gov/feg/current.shtml. In the long term, fuel cell–powered vehicles that run on hydrogen and produce no pollution whatsoever could provide an answer to our oil addiction. Unfortunately, they are not available now, and the technology is so complex that they will probably not be mass produced for at least another 15–20 years.

Trains, Planes or Automobiles?

The Dirty Secret of the Skies: If you're planning a long trip, the mode of transport you use can have a big impact on the environment. The worst choice, at least as far as our planet is concerned, is flying. Air travel is already responsible for 8 percent of our greenhouse gas emissions—in spite of the fact that far fewer people fly regularly than use cars. Planes might have revolutionized travel, but they also generate huge amounts of carbon dioxide and other harmful pollutants such as sulfur and nitrous oxide. An average flight between the east and west coasts of the United States produces a massive three to four tons of carbon dioxide for every single person on the plane! Of course, sometimes you'll need to fly. But it is worth checking out the alternatives, especially if you're not traveling too far.

Why Trains Are So Good . . . : One option is the train. If you are just traveling a few hundred miles, it can often be as quick (or quicker) than taking a plane. In the United States, high-speed Acela trains now operate between Boston, New York and Washington, D.C. Even in areas of the country where fast trains are not yet available, rail services can still provide a good travel option. For instance, if you're planning a trip from Chicago to Saint Louis, it can take as little as five-and-a-half hours on the train to travel the 300 miles between the two cities. A flight can actually take nearly as long when you factor in the longer check-in times and security procedures introduced into our airports since 9/11. Many airports are also more remote and can take longer to reach than central train stations. The train is often a lot cheaper, too. Meanwhile, in many parts of Europe, Canada and Japan, fast and efficient train services are extremely common.

. . . and Buses Are Better: When it comes to climate change, a train is almost always superior to a plane. But a bus is often even better. These days, long-distance bus services like Greyhound in the United States (www.greyhound.com) or National Express in Britain offer a pleasant alternative to planes and trains. In many cases, they are even less harmful in terms of overall fossil fuel emissions than trains—and far, far better than planes, causing just one-sixth of the pollution per passenger. They are often much, much cheaper, too. For example, a trip between New York and Washington, D.C., can take as little as four hours and twenty minutes and cost as little as $22. Trips from Dallas to Houston are almost as quick and inexpensive, while a journey from San Diego to Los Angeles can take less than two-and-a-half hours and set you back just $15.

HOME IMPROVEMENTS

Some money-saving measures are so easy you don't even need to step outside your front door. The average household racks up over $1,300 in electricity bills each year, and every room holds at least half-a-dozen energy-conserving secrets that could save you money. If just 1 percent of Americans started to practice energy efficiency in their homes, together we would have made a huge difference to the amount of greenhouse gases the country emits, and taken a big step forward in the battle against climate change. That's because most of the electricity generated in the United States comes from power stations that run on coal, gas or oil, the main culprits behind the greenhouse gases responsible for climate change.

Conquering Your Kitchen

Refrigerators, cookers, dishwashers and other kitchen appliances are big electricity consumers, and all will happily pile on the pounds when it comes to your electricity bill. The good news, though, is that there are some easy ways to stop these power-hungry machines from eating into your earnings.

Fridge: Take your fridge, for example. It's the biggest single energy user in many homes, costing the average family well over $100 each year to run. But in just sixty seconds, you could halve that. For a start, most fridges are on a colder setting than they need to be. Check your fridge's thermostat (you should find it on the inside door). If it's set lower than 37°F then it's too cold. Even at 40°F, your food and drinks will be kept chilly enough for anyone's tastes. Now take a look at your freezer setting. This doesn't need to be colder than 4°F—setting it lower won't make your food any healthier. But it will cost you a whole lot more money. And take longer for items to defrost. If your fridge has number settings but doesn't indicate temperatures (some fridges have cold settings of, say, 1–5 or 1–10), you can still save energy. Try turning it down a couple of notches onto a slightly warmer setting—you shouldn't detect any difference in the temperature of your food, but you will notice a change in your monthly bill.

Another energy-saving option is to position your fridge away from your cooker and heaters, if possible, as this will mean it is in a cooler environment and won't have to work so hard. In summer, make sure the fridge isn't in direct sunlight, as this heats it up and forces it to work harder, too.

Next, take a look at your fridge's condenser coils—they're the coils that you'll find at the back of most fridges, usually at the bottom (if you can't find yours, check the manual). If the coils look dusty, it means they are having to work harder to cool your fridge. Try gently vacuuming them, or cleaning them with a cloth or brush. Congratulations! You've just improved your fridge's energy efficiency by as much as one third. Do this a couple of times a year, and you could slice $20–30 from your power bills.

If you have a second fridge or freezer in the basement or elsewhere, it's worth giving a moment's thought to whether you actually need it. Some of us use these to store extra food we buy on sale. Unfortunately, though, the cost of running a second fridge or freezer is often a lot more than the money you save on what you're storing inside it. It is far better for your budget to have just one efficient fridge-freezer.

Finally, if you're thinking of buying a new fridge, you're in luck—most of the latest models are far more efficient than their predecessors of five or ten years ago. Some new fridges are definitely better than others, though, so the choice you make can mean hundreds of dollars' difference in your energy bills over the long term. The U.S. government has set up an energy rating system that will tell you which models are best. It's called Energy Star and you can read about it at www.energystar.gov. Appliances that rate highly under the Energy Star program will save you hundreds or even thousands of dollars over the lifetime of the product. For instance, a new refrigerator endorsed by Energy Star will save you up to $70 a year compared with many older fridges. That's more than $1,000 saved over the 15 years you can expect your new appliance to last. Give some thought to the size of the fridge you really need, too—the larger the unit, the more electricity it usually consumes. The American Council for an Energy-Efficient Economy provides an easy-to-use guide to the best fridges and freezers: www.aceee. org/consumerguide/topfridge.htm.

Dishwasher: Dishwashers are another energy hog. Luckily, though, there are a few easy ways to stop them from making a pig of themselves with your energy bills. For a start, try to only run your dishwasher when it's full (or nearly full). Most of the energy your dishwasher needs comes from the hot water it uses, and as the water used each cycle stays the same regardless of how full the machine is, you should wash more items rather than less. Also, try using the shortest cycle possible. Most machines have a "light wash" or energy-saving setting that will do the job just as well as any other option. And if your machine has an "air dry" setting, use it in preference to "heat dry" or any other alternatives—it means your dishwasher won't expend extra energy sucking in and heating up air from outside to dry your dishes, but will instead use the warm air already in the dryer. If your dishwasher doesn't have this, try stopping the cycle as it reaches the drying stage. Then open the door and let the dishes dry naturally. It might take a little longer, but it will cut your bills by $30 or more every year. Finally, if you're thinking of buying a new dishwasher, make sure you buy a model that's approved by the Energy Star scheme—it could save as much as $25 each year to run when compared with your old washer.

Oven: You can save money by changing your cooking habits, too—and no, it's not by only eating salads. For a start, if your oven has a convection fan, use it. By circulating the air in your oven, the food will cook more rapidly. Next, try replacing your metal pans with glass or ceramic ones—they hold heat a lot more effectively, and will quicken your cooking time, too. Putting lids on your pans will help as well. Finally, quit looking in the oven every five minutes! Every time you do, a quarter of the heat slips out. If you're in the market for a new gas oven or range, find one that has an automatic electric ignition system, as it means the pilot light won't have to burn all the time.

Microwave and Toaster Oven: Microwaves are generally a lot more energy efficient than traditional ovens, especially when it comes to reheating food and basic cooking. So are toaster ovens, pressure cookers, and even your stove top, especially if you're making smaller meals. Try using these instead of your oven whenever possible.

Cleaning Up in the Laundry

Washing Machine: Money laundering might be a bad thing, but saving money on your laundry certainly isn't. For a start, did you know that warm or cold wash cycles are just as good as hot at cleaning your clothes? They are also much, much cheaper. Using a cold wash will cut your washing machine costs by more than half. Modern detergents are so good nowadays that it really doesn't matter what temperature water is going into the machine. So, unless your clothes are really dirty, try using a cold wash. Your garments will come out just as clean and you'll save money with your laundering—all without breaking a single law. Also, try not to do your washing until you have enough for a full load. Two half-empty loads are far less efficient. Don't overload the machine, though, as this could mean your clothes don't get washed properly. As with any other appliance, if you're in the market for a new one, make sure you buy a model that's approved by the Energy Star scheme.

Dryer: Clothes dryers are a major expense for most households, racking up close to $100 each year for the average family. Obviously, the best way to save money on this expensive appliance is to line dry your clothes. It's absolutely free! Sometimes this won't be practical, though—for instance, if it's cold or wet outside, or if you live in an apartment (although an indoor drying rack could still come in handy on occasions). When you do use your dryer, you can save money by avoiding overdrying your clothes—if you set the dryer for 90 minutes but most loads are dry after 60, that's a lot of wasted electricity. Some dryers now have moisture sensors that stop the machine as soon as your clothes are dry. If you have a moisture sensor, you should use it—it will cut your annual bill by about $15. Also, make sure you clean the lint trap regularly, as this will improve your dryer's efficiency. Finally, you'll notice that some types of fabrics dry faster than others. Towels or woolen clothes, for instance, take longer. Try separating these from faster-drying items. And don't add wet clothes to a load that's already half-dry, as it will slow down the drying process considerably.

Beat Those Bathroom Blues

On average, Americans use over 45 gallons of hot water every day in the bathroom alone. The biggest culprits are your shower and your sink. When it comes to your shower, there are two easy options. The first is to spend a little less time in there. While a long, hot shower can feel great, every minute you spend in there consumes up to 6 gallons of hot water. Cutting your shower time just slightly, say from 8 to 6 minutes, will therefore save as much as 4,400 gallons of hot water each year. A second option is to buy a new showerhead at your local hardware store. If your showerhead is more than 10 years old, chances are it's using a lot more water than it should. Modern showerheads are designed to use a lot less water while giving you the same water pressure. That's because newer showerheads add air to the water. It feels the same as those powerful old showerheads, but uses 1–2 gallons per minute—far less than its technologically challenged predecessors. New showerheads cost less than $20, and are generally easy to install. Better still, it will pay for itself within three or four months, shaving several dollars off every power bill. Meanwhile, if you're big on baths, try to cut down a little. Taking a shower is almost always lighter on the hot water, especially if it's not too long.

As for your sink, saving is even easier. First, remember to turn the tap off when you're brushing your teeth or shaving. Just one minute of hot water from your faucet will run up to three gallons of hot water down the drain. Next, take a minute to fix those leaky taps with your trusty wrench; each one you tighten up can stop as much as a gallon a day in lost water.

An Efficient Home Office

Desktop Computer: Want to make your home office as efficient as it can be? You can cut costs and downsize your power bill with a couple of simple steps. Let's start with your computer. If you've been leaving it turned on all the time because you heard that switching it on and off a lot is bad for it, then you've been misled. Hard drives these days are designed to be switched on and off. They will actually last longer if they get some downtime, too. So forget about the screensaver and the "sleep" option, turn your computer hard drive and monitor off when you're done with them and you'll soon be cost-cutting as effectively as any company office—all from the comfort of your own home.

Printer: Now, let's turn to your printer. This can gobble up energy as well, so if you're not using it, turn it off. Try cutting down on your paper use, too. Unless it's an important document, try using both sides of the page. It will save on your paper and energy bills. If you are considering buying a printer, look at the inkjet option. While they're slower than laserjets, they're much, much cheaper and use just a fraction of the electricity. These days, the print quality of new inkjets is just as good as most laserjets, too.

Laptop: Finally, if you've decided it is time to replace your old desktop computer, think about buying a laptop. Not only will you get to work while hanging out in Starbucks with your latest high-tech fashion accessory, you'll also cut down on your energy bills, as laptops are up to 90 percent more energy efficient than desktop computers. It could cut as much as $30 from your annual energy bill.

See the Light

Your light bulbs are burning a hole in your pocket, or more accurately, in your electricity bill. But you can improve their use without even raising a sweat. The first step is the easiest—just turn the light off when you leave a room (unless there is someone else still in there, of course). You may have heard that keeping a light on all the time is better for the bulb and uses less energy than turning it on and off. It's a myth, and it's costing you money. With just two fewer lights on in the evenings, you can shave another three bucks from your monthly power bill. It may not sound like much, but it quickly adds up.

A second step is to change your light bulbs. Most Americans are still using old-fashioned incandescent bulbs. These have been around since the Ark (well, since the nineteenth century, anyway). As it is old technology, they are cheap to produce, but very inefficient, producing more heat than light—which is not much use to you unless you're crazy enough to be using your light bulbs to stay warm. In short, old incandescent bulbs are cheap to buy, but expensive to run.

Nowadays, though, there is an alternative—the compact fluorescent light. It is more expensive to buy (around $15). But in the long run, it will save you a lot of money. That's because it lasts for 10,000 hours, ten times longer than the old incandescent bulbs, which often splutter and die after just 1,000 hours. The new bulbs are also much more efficient—for instance, a 25-watt compact fluorescent light is as bright as one of your old 100-watt incandescent bulbs—which means it will cost you only a quarter as much to run. So, when one of your old bulbs runs out, try a compact fluorescent bulb—they're for sale in your grocery or hardware store next to the regular ones. It might cost you a few dollars more to start with, but in the long run, each one you buy will save you $50 on your energy bills over the lifetime of the bulb.

OD-ing on the A/C

Air conditioning—it's a life saver! Three out of four Americans use it in their homes. Not that this should come as much of a surprise. It makes life bearable during those long, hot summers, beating back even the most sweltering heat wave and leaving us to relax in that sweet, cool air that we'd otherwise only experience on the most perfect spring or fall days. The downside to this coolest of inventions, though, is the heat it puts on us when we receive our monthly energy bill. Most families spend close to $200 each year on their A/C. Fortunately, there are a few simple tips you can use to help put the freeze on rising power bills—and on global warming—while allowing you to keep your cool this summer.

First, clean the filter. Dirty filters make your A/C a lot less efficient. If your filter looks dirty, change it. You can buy replacements at your hardware store—a disposable filter will set you back about a buck, while filters that can be washed and reused cost a bit more (but are less expensive in the long run). Next, clean the A/C's coils. These are covered by little fins, and they collect a lot of dirt or dust. Wiping them down so they're clean will mean your A/C won't have to work so hard to cool your room.

Also, if you have a central air conditioner for the whole house (rather than a room air conditioner that fits in the window), try changing the setting to a slightly less cold temperature. After all, how cool do you really want to be? And if your A/C has a setting that allows you to recirculate the air already in the room (rather than pulling air in from outside), try using it. It means the air it is cooling is not so hot, which makes its task a lot easier, and saves on electricity.

If you are using a room air conditioner, remember to close doors behind you so cool air doesn't escape elsewhere. And if you're not planning on spending time in a particular room for a while, don't waste your money cooling it. It also pays to have your A/C system professionally serviced every few years—an expert can service your A/C, tell you if there is still enough refrigerating fluid, and check that everything is in proper working order. If you are buying a new A/C, make sure you buy a model that's approved by the Energy Star scheme. The more efficient units will cut your on-going costs considerably.

Fans: Another option is to use a fan instead. This is useful on days that are not too hot. Fans move air and create a breeze that helps our bodies cool down almost as well as an A/C (unless temperatures are extremely high). The best type is the ceiling fan, although smaller portable fans or the fans on most A/C units also work pretty well. If you use fans instead of your A/C one day out of three over the summer months, you'll shave about $50 from your seasonal electricity bills.

Coolers: Swamp coolers—or evaporative coolers as they're also known—are another alternative if you live in a place that gets dry heat (such as the Southwest), although they don't work well in humid climates. Evaporative coolers use a less technologically advanced system than A/Cs, cooling the air by sucking it through moist pads. Even so, such coolers are pretty effective, reducing temperatures by around 20°F. They are also much cheaper to run than the average A/C, using just a quarter of the electricity demanded by your power-hungry air conditioner. Coolers are cheaper to buy, too, with many models costing from $100 to $200. Before you start shopping for one, though, be warned. While they're great in places that experience dry heat, they really don't work well in areas that suffer from too much humidity (so don't bother trying them in Washington, D.C., or Miami, for instance).

Cut Heating Costs, No Sweat!

Home Heating System: Most households in the United States have a centralized home heating system run by a boiler or furnace. The newer the system, the more efficient it is likely to be. But whatever age it is, your home heating system can almost certainly be made to run better and cost less over those winter months. For a start, make sure you regularly clean and vacuum the heating vents around your home, and check that they're not blocked or covered by furniture, rugs, your heat-seeking pets or anything else that might stop the system working properly. Also, try to replace the filter once a month—dust-filled furnace filters force the system to work harder to distribute the same amount of heat. If you've had it a while, you might even want to consider having an expert take a look at your heating system to see if it's functioning optimally. They should check the ducts that transport the heat around your home, too (most older ducts are leaky and need to be resealed).

Your electricity company should be able to recommend someone, or will have their own technician. If you are something of a home handyman or -woman, you could even try taking a look at the furnace and ducts yourself. Visit www.homeenergy.org/consumer-info/ducts for more hands-on advice.

You can also use the heating system's thermostat to your advantage. First, try turning the temperature down a little during the winter months—trimming it by just 3°F will cut your heating bill by about 6 percent. If you have a programmable thermostat, take a few minutes to figure out how it works—it could save you a lot of money. For instance, you could program it to work less hard while everyone is out at work or school, or to be a little cooler at night when you're all asleep. And if you are not using a room for a while, turn off the radiators, close the heating vents, or turn down the thermostat (if you have one) for that room. Why waste money warming an empty space?

Curtains, Caulking, Windows and Weather Stripping: One of the big costs with any home heating system comes from replacing the heat lost out of the house. By making sure you close your curtains or blinds at night, you'll help prevent heat loss through the windows. You should also consider weather stripping your windows and front and back doors if they are letting in too much of a draft or if you can see gaps around them that let the light through. Weather strips are placed around the edges of windows and exterior doors to cut down on heat loss. They're cheap and available from any hardware store. You could also try caulking your windows and doors. Caulk is a sealant used to fill gaps and make your home watertight—it usually looks like a thin strip of white, slightly rubbery material about a quarter-inch wide that's often placed around your bathtub or wash basin. But it can also be used to make your windows and doors more airtight. Caulking is even less expensive than weather stripping. Just a few minutes making your windows and exterior doors a little less leaky and windy could cut several dollars from your monthly power bill. Caulk does need replacing every couple of years, though. For more information visit: http://doity-ourself.com/windows/more.htm or www.eere.energy.gov/con-sumerinfo/factsheets/weatherize.html.

It is also worth considering whether you could use some new windows. If your windows have just a single pane of glass—and about half of American homes and apartments do—you could benefit a lot from upgrading to double-pane windows. While it can be quite costly in the short term, energy-efficient windows will cut your expenses a lot over the long run.

Insulation: One of the best ways to save on your heating costs is to have a well-insulated home. Unfortunately, most homes are not properly insulated. According to a study published in 2004, two-thirds of American homes are under-insulated. A poorly insulated home will lose heat through its walls, floors and ceilings far faster than it needs to, heaping as much as $150 in additional costs onto your annual energy bills. In most cases, the more insulation your home has, the better. Insulation won't just reduce your costs, either—it can even help cut out a lot of outside street sounds, and can filter the noise that passes between the rooms in your house. The best places to work on are your attic, basement, ceilings and exterior walls. The attic is probably the smartest place to start, because it's the source of a lot of heat loss, and does not require a professional to install—meaning you may be able to do it yourself and save on installation costs. Insulation can come in various shapes and sizes, including "batts" (which usually look like oversize, slightly furry pink bricks), as well as "rolls" or "blankets." These are all commonly used in attics. There are also rigid foam boards that are usually placed in walls and basements. Whatever shape it takes, though, most insulation is made from either fiberglass (a mixture of sand and recycled glass) or rock wool (which comes from basaltic rock and recycled waste from steel mills).

Don't be fooled, though. Just because most insulation is made from the same stuff does not make it all equal when it comes to keeping your home nice and snug. Some insulation traps considerably more heat than others. Fortunately, these days it is easy to tell how much insulation you'll get by checking a product's "R-value." This rating should appear on the packaging. The higher the R-value, the more heat-trapping potential you are getting. For instance, insulation that is rated at a lowly R–8 provides relatively limited amounts of insulation, while an R–49 product means you can expect to prevent a lot more heat loss. To find out more about insulating your home (or adding more insulation), visit the North American Insulation Manufacturers Association online guide to home insulation (www.simplyinsulate.com) or try the U.S. Energy Department's site (www.ornl.gov/sci/roofs+walls/insulation).

Get Into (and Out of) Hot Water

Your water heater gives your major appliances a run for their money—or should that be *your* money?—when it comes to consuming energy. Only the fridge is more expensive. Luckily, though, a few easy steps can help control your hot water bills. That's because most water heaters are set to make your precious H_2O far hotter than it needs to be. Many are programmed as high as 140°F. There is no reason for this. Check the thermostat: if it's that high, try dropping it down to 130°F or 120°F (note: your dishwasher might require a hotter setting, but most have their own heating unit to do this). Also, check if your water heater has insulation (usually a silver-colored "jacket" around it). If it does not you should be able to find one in your local hardware store for about $10–15. They are easy to install and will pay for themselves in less than a year. And look at the hot water pipes to see if they have insulation, too. If your heater has a timer, try turning off the hot water during the night. But don't forget to make sure it's switched back on 30–45 minutes before you want to use it for your morning shower.

New Water Heaters: While the tips suggested above will definitely help rein in your hot water bills, there is a way to save even more money. If your water heater is more than a few years old, it is worth considering buying a new one. In the long run, it will save you a lot. New federal standards set in 2004 on energy efficiency for water heaters mean that any new heater will be more efficient than what you have now, and will save you a lot of money. Bear in mind, though, that if you have the option of choosing a natural gas, oil or propane water heater, these are often cheaper to run than electric models.

It is also worth considering what size water heater you really need, as this can obviously make a big difference to your ongoing costs. As a general rule, the smaller your place and the fewer the people living there, the smaller the water heater you'll need. If there are just a couple of you and it is a one bedroom place, for instance, a 30–40 gallon heater will probably satisfy your needs. On the other hand, if there are five or six of you living in a larger place, you should consider a 60, 66 or even 80 gallon unit. For additional advice on how to go about choosing your new water heater, visit www.eere.energy.gov/consumerinfo/ and follow the link to "water heating."

Geothermal Heaters: Although the modern electric or gas water heaters described above are much more energy efficient than their predecessors, there are other alternatives that could save you even more. One of the most environmentally friendly options is the geothermal heat pump, a small device that extracts heat from below the ground by your home (temperatures are more consistent throughout the year a few feet underground). Also known as the "earth-source" or "ground-source" heat pump, these heaters will cost upward of $1,000 to install but will slash your annual energy bills by at least $80. For more information, visit www.eere.energy.gov/consumerinfo/ and follow the link to "geothermal heat pumps."

Solar Heating and Solar Power: Another alternative that is now very cost-effective is solar heating. That's because, once they're installed, solar heating panels are virtually free! After all, they are fed by sunlight. It is also very user-friendly these days, as the technology has developed a lot in recent years. There are two types of solar power that are popular these days. The first is the solar water heater. This employs panels installed on your roof that capture the sun's heat and turn it into hot water. Solar water heaters usually cost around $2,000 to install, but will last up to 25 years. During that time, though, you will cut your energy bill by $100–150 or more each and every year. Solar heating can also warm your pool, potentially saving you hundreds of dollars a year. For more information on solar heating, visit www.eere.energy.gov/consumerinfo and click on the link to "solar water heaters."

While solar water heaters are an increasingly popular option, it is worth remembering that they provide only hot water, and not electricity. A second, more advanced solar power alternative is the photovoltaic cell. These cells use modern technology to convert the Sun's light directly into electricity. Photovoltaic cells are more expensive than solar water heaters to start with, but have the big advantage of supplying free electricity—and not just hot water—throughout your home. For more information, visit www.eere.energy.gov/consumerinfo and click on the link to "photovoltaics."

Many states and some electricity utilities offer tax credits, subsidies, loans or grants to install solar water heaters, photovoltaic cells or other environmentally friendly energy sources. To help you make a decision on whether to install solar power or some other environmentally friendly option, the Interstate Renewable Energy Council and North Carolina Solar Center have developed a website showing what support is available in your state (www.dsireusa.org). If you need further information or advice, try your state tax or energy office or local electric company. Unfortunately, no federal programs currently exist, although this may change in the future.

Energy Audit Your Home

If you have introduced some of the energy conservation measures suggested above, you're already well on your way to cutting your home electricity bills by several hundred dollars each year. But perhaps you'd like to take things a step further, and would love some more advice about additional cost-cutting tips specifically tailored to your particular home or apartment? If so, then an energy "audit" could be a smart move. An energy audit will help identify specific ways to conserve energy that are customized to your dwelling and location. Because every house, condo or apartment is different, an energy audit will help pinpoint any particular problems that are specific to your residence. Knowing exactly where your dwelling falls short of perfection on the energy front could add even more to the money you save on your annual bills.

"Do-It-Yourself" Audits: The easiest (and cheapest) way to carry out a home energy audit is to do one for yourself. Grab a pen and paper and make a careful inspection of the entire house. First, check every room for drafts. As noted earlier in the chapter, air leaks often show up around windows and doors, and can be dealt with by caulking or weather stripping. But you can also find leaks in a multitude of other places, such as around the edge of the flooring, through fireplace dampers, mail slots and air conditioning units. Check the outside of the building for cracks and air leaks, too, especially the corners of the structure, as well as areas where the pipes, faucets and wiring enter or exit the house. You should also check how much insulation you have; in general, the older the house, the less you can expect. Start with the attic, basement, water heater, pipes and furnace ducts. Make sure your heating and cooling equipment is in good condition, too. For further guidance on how to carry out your own energy audit, visit the government's advice page: http://www.eere.energy.gov/consumer-info/factsheets/ea2.html.

Professional Audits: A second option is to call in a professional. While this will obviously cost more, it will be more thorough, and could help you identify problems you might not notice. An energy specialist should spend several hours making a careful examination of every room, as well as the exterior of the house. A good auditor may also use infrared cameras or other hi-tech equipment, and should ask you for your previous electricity and gas bills. They will probably use a powerful fan called a "blower door" to check for air leaks. To help the auditor, try to alert them to any problems you've noticed, for instance if one part of the house feels too hot or cold, or gets more condensation or mildew.

To find a reliable energy auditor, ask your state or local government energy office or your local utility company. Most should be able to recommend one. Some may even offer their own expert at a subsidized rate. The National Association of Energy Service Companies (www.naesco.org) may also be able to help out. Before you hire an auditor, though, make sure you get them to quote you a price, and shop around, if you can, as prices can vary considerably.

Online Audits: If you don't want to pay for a professional audit but are reluctant to do it all by yourself, an online audit could be the way to go. There are several helpful websites offering free online audits. By responding to some simple questions about your home, the appliances you use and so on, these sites provide information and advice on how you can conserve more energy and save on your power bills. The Energy Guide site (www.energyguide.com) provides both a fast-track and a more in-depth analysis of your home's energy use. Another excellent option is the Home Energy Saver website (http://hes.lbl.gov), which is sponsored by the U.S. Energy Department and Environmental Protection Agency.

Clean, Green Electricity

Oil, gas and coal-fired power stations are responsible for so much of the world's global warming problem that it should come as no surprise that most of the tips and suggestions in this chapter are focused on finding ways to save electricity. Reducing energy use around our homes, offices and elsewhere is a great way to help combat global warming. But while controlling your energy use is one of the best ways you can help, it's important to know that not all electricity is bad. In recent years, some electricity has started to come from sources that do not contribute to global warming. These sources, such as wind, solar, hydro (water) or geothermal power, do not release fossil fuels into the atmosphere, so don't cause global warming or air pollution. Such sources of electricity are often referred to as "renewable" or "green" energy. While they still only account for a tiny percentage of the total electricity being produced, their contribution is increasing as each year passes.

As a consumer, you now have the choice of buying your electricity specifically from these sources rather than from the highly polluting coal, oil or gas power stations. In recent years, a growing number of utilities have started to produce and offer green energy as an option to their customers. While it differs state by state, consumers in many parts of the country can now join "green power pricing programs," which allow you to buy your electricity from environmentally friendly sources. For more information on green power in your state, visit www.eere.energy.gov/greenpower/buying or www.green-e.org.

Buyer Beware: Before you decide to leap into the world of green power, though, a word of warning. Unlike all the other suggestions in this chapter, this one will not save you a cent. Actually, it will end up costing you more! This is because green electricity is still slightly more expensive than energy generated from fossil fuel power stations. For a start, the technology is newer and more advanced, meaning the costs have not had much of a chance to fall to the level of "old" energy sources such as oil and coal. For this reason, green energy is not a money-saving option at this stage, and is not recommended as something you should consider if you are on a tight budget. So, while buying green power would certainly support utilities that are taking climate change seriously, and would send a message to the others that they need to shape up, it is not suggested for those on a limited budget—at least not right now.

Looking further ahead, the news is a lot better. The price of green energy is continuing to fall, so over time the cost differences should disappear, meaning you will eventually be able to buy green energy at the same price as any other electricity. Ultimately, it should cost even less. In the meantime, you have all the other measures outlined in this chapter to choose from that will allow you to help combat global warming while also saving you plenty of money.

YOUR YARD AND GARDEN

Become a Tree Hugger (and Planter)

Plants and trees are the perfect antiwarming antidote. Every tree, shrub, bush or vine you plant around your home directly helps in the fight against climate change. That's because plants soak up carbon dioxide—the very thing that's causing global warming. The average tree soaks up a *ton* of carbon over its life, reversing some of the damage done by our cars, homes, offices and factories. Better still, landscaping your garden in the right way can actually help save on your power bills. For instance, if you can shade your air conditioner from direct sunlight by placing, say, a couple of shrubs a few feet away, your A/C won't have to work so hard. Planting trees that shade your home during summer, or act as a windbreak in winter, can also help cut cooling and heating costs. Deciduous trees, which shed their leaves in the fall, are ideal, because they shade your house from the hot sun in summer, but let the light through their empty branches in winter. Trees and plants also naturally cool the area around them by up to 10°F because of photosynthesis (the plant equivalent of eating and breathing). This means your house will benefit from the cooling effect over the summer. And you don't have to shift giant trees into your garden for it to work—even a small sapling can make a difference. For more on how to make your garden go to work on your power bills, visit: www.eere.energy.gov/consumer-info/energy_savers/landscaping.html.

Convert to Composting

Composting is a great way to help yourself while also helping the environment. Most of us put out "organic" trash such as fruit and vegetables, used paper towels, coffee filters, old leaves or lint from the clothes dryer or vacuum cleaner in our regular garbage. This organic trash consists of materials that decompose easily. The problem is that this type of material is a nightmare in our landfills. Because landfills compact their garbage, these organic substances are tightly compressed, which makes them decompose in a way that releases a substance called methane—a major greenhouse gas second only to carbon dioxide in terms of how much it is contributing to global warming. The problem is so great that, in the United States, two-fifths of total methane emissions come from our landfills.

Composting in your own garden helps prevent these methane emissions by allowing these organic materials to decompose more naturally. It can also cut down on your regular trash by as much as one-third, saving you money if you live in a place where you pay for your garbage disposal by the bag. It's the most natural type of recycling there is. Plus, composting creates high-quality fertilizer that any gardening enthusiast will love.

Making Your Compost Pile: Creating a compost pile in your garden is not difficult. While there are several types of composting, the easiest is known as "cold pile" composting. Your first step is to decide where to place your compost pile. In general, your pile should be placed at least two feet from any structure such as a house or wall. Many people find that a location in the garden that's a little distance from the house is best. Try not to make it too far, though, as you will have to take your kitchen waste to the pile, and so don't want it to be inconvenient. Some people prefer to buy a proper compost bin. While it is not absolutely necessary (you can put your pile on the ground if you prefer), it does keep the pile under control and helps it look neat and tidy. Whether you decide to buy a compost bin or not, many people like to place their pile in some quiet, flat corner of the garden that is at least partly shaded, and where it is not too obvious. Having a compost pile in the middle of the lawn isn't generally desirable.

Once you've decided where to place the pile, you can start putting your organic waste there. Try and make sure you have a mix of materials, from grass and leaves to food waste (but not meat or dairy waste). A combination of different types of waste helps the materials decompose more quickly and effectively. There are two major kinds of materials needed for the compost pile to work best—those that are rich in nitrogen, and those that are heavy in carbon. The nitrogen-endowed materials, which some experts call "greens," include grass, weeds, old fruit and vegetables, tea bags and coffee filters. The carbon-rich items, which are also called "browns," include fallen leaves, ash from your fireplace and lint from your vacuum cleaner or dryer. Ensuring there's a mix of these two different types of materials will lead to the most effective composting. As an added extra that will help even more, you should make sure your fruit and vegetable waste is hidden under some other materials, as this will keep the bugs away.

Eureka! You now have a compost pile. Add to the pile whenever you like, and try turning it with a pitchfork or shovel every few weeks to make sure the compost is getting enough oxygen. After a few months, fully decomposed compost—or humus—will begin to appear at the bottom of the pile. This should look like a dark, crumbly, rich and rather woody-smelling soil. As any avid gardener will tell you, it's superb for helping your plants grow, either in the garden or as a potting mix.

Hot vs. Cold Composting: If you want to get more scientific about composting in order to make the waste decompose more quickly, you can always move from "cold" to "hot pile" composting. This basically involves a few more steps and a little more work, as well as requiring a bit more precision about how much of each type of waste you add to your pile. Hot pile composting results in higher temperatures within the pile, which is a good thing because it hastens the process of decomposition. For a simple guide on how to do it, visit the U.S. Agriculture Department's site www.nrcs.usda.gov/feature/backyard/ or http://vegweb.com/composting/.

Don't Turn It into Trash—Recycle!

Recycling is one of the best things you can do to combat climate change. It takes far less electricity to recycle than to make something from new. And it creates a lot of jobs. Although many people already recycle, we can do more. A lot more. In spite of the introduction of recycling schemes across the United States, we're still tossing out more garbage than ever before. The average American currently throws away more than four pounds of trash every single day, or 1,600 pounds of the stuff each year. That's double what it was in the 1970s. More than 21 *billion* plastic bottles are thrown out rather than recycled each year just in the United States—the equivalent of 70 bottles from every man, woman and child in the country. And we're only talking plastic here. There are also vast amounts of paper, glass and aluminum and steel cans that can be recycled, not to mention used motor oil, old car tires and even batteries. Would you believe that we use 18 billion disposable diapers each year?

The result is that, in the United States alone, we produce eight *tons* of trash every second! That's around 50 tons more trash added to the pile in the time it took you to read the last two sentences—unless you like to read slowly, in which case it's even more. A whopping 80 percent of this garbage could be recycled. Sadly, most of it isn't. Less than one-third of our garbage is recycled, while nearly two-thirds still ends up on the landfill.

Americans could make a real difference to this problem, too, because although we have just 5 percent of the world's population, we produce 40 percent of the trash. We're ten times more wasteful than our neighbors in Central America, and even two or three times worse than the French. It's been estimated that recycling America's paper products alone could save up to one *billion* trees every year. Imagine the impact this would have on combating global warming.

When it comes to our trash, then, every one of us really *can* make a difference. Recycling our cans, bottles, newspapers and plastic would slash greenhouse gas emissions by the equivalent of 900 pounds of carbon dioxide per year for each and every household. Most states now collect recyclable materials alongside your regular trash—or at least have recycling collection points. Some places even give you money back when you return glass or plastic bottles or aluminum cans. So, next time you're taking out the trash, stop a moment and consider what's going to be taken to the landfill, and what could be recycled. For more information on how to go about recycling where you live, visit: www.epa.gov/epaoswer/non-hw/muncpl/faq.htm#11.

ENERGY SAVER CHECKLIST

Around the Home

- ❑ When buying a new appliance, find the most energy efficient at www.energystar.com
- ❑ Carry out a home energy audit
- ❑ Turn off the lights when you're not using a room
- ❑ Buy new compact fluorescent bulbs when your old-fashioned bulbs stop working
- ❑ Consider a new geothermal or solar water heater
- ❑ Turn down the thermostat on your water heater from 140°F to 120–130°F
- ❑ Place insulation around your water heater
- ❑ Install/use a timer on the water heater
- ❑ Clean the filters on your A/C
- ❑ Turn your A/C temperature setting down
- ❑ On warm (but not extremely hot) days, use a fan rather than A/C
- ❑ In winter, turn the thermostat down a little on your home heating system

- ❏ Use weather stripping and caulking to prevent heat loss from your windows and exterior doors
- ❏ Insulate your home
- ❏ Replace the furnace filter once a month
- ❏ Vacuum around the home heating vents

Kitchen

- ❏ Turn your fridge's thermostat onto a slightly warmer setting
- ❏ Clean the coils on your fridge
- ❏ Buy an energy-efficient fridge
- ❏ Use your oven's convection fan when cooking
- ❏ Put a lid on your pans
- ❏ Switch from metal to ceramic or glass pans
- ❏ Don't keep opening the oven door to check on your food
- ❏ Use your microwave, toaster oven or pressure cooker ahead of your electric oven

Laundry

- ❏ Use a cold (or warm) wash cycle instead of a hot one
- ❏ Line dry your clothes instead of using a dryer
- ❏ When using your dryer, avoid overdrying
- ❏ Use the dryer's moisture sensor (if it has one)
- ❏ Clean out the dryer's lint trap regularly

Bathroom

- ❏ Fix your leaky faucets
- ❏ Don't let the hot water run when you're not using it
- ❏ Install a low-flow showerhead
- ❏ Cut down on long showers

Home Office

- ❏ Turn off your computer, monitor and printer when you are not using them

- ❏ Replace your old desktop computer with a laptop
- ❏ Consider an inkjet printer over a laserjet model
- ❏ Try to use less printer paper (and print on both sides when possible)

In Your Yard and Garden

- ❏ Shade your house with plants and trees
- ❏ Start composting
- ❏ Cut down on your garbage
- ❏ Recycle your plastic, aluminum and steel cans, paper and glass

On the Road

- ❏ Give your car a regular tune-up
- ❏ Check that your tires are inflated properly
- ❏ Cut down on your car use
- ❏ Use public transport or carpooling
- ❏ Try walking or biking
- ❏ On long trips, take the train or intercity bus instead of flying
- ❏ Buy a more fuel-efficient car or a hybrid vehicle
- ❏ Shop online instead of driving to the store
- ❏ Telecommute

Shopping

- ❏ Buy from and invest in climate-friendly "green" companies
- ❏ Eat more locally grown food
- ❏ Buy organic fruit and vegetables
- ❏ Bring your own shopping bag
- ❏ Eat a little less meat, especially red meat
- ❏ Do not buy bottled water—purchase a filter instead
- ❏ Use a filter instead of a watercooler
- ❏ Sell or donate your second-hand goods

THE END . . . OR THE BEGINNING?

Climate change is probably the greatest threat facing humanity in the twenty-first century. It is certainly the world's worst environmental threat, as Tony Blair warned in a major speech delivered in September 2004.

The threat is with us now. Already, it kills an estimated 150,000 people around the world each year. To put that into perspective, that is 50 times the number who lost their lives on 9/11, and 250 times more than the combined total of U.S. and allied troops killed in Iraq in the first 12 months following the 2003 invasion and defeat of Saddam Hussein. Right now, most of the 150,000 who die each year from the effects of global warming live in the Third World. But climate change is rapidly making its presence felt everywhere. Soon, nowhere will be immune.

You may not know it yet, but global warming is already beginning to intrude into your life, whether you're a resident of Bangalore, Berlin, or even Birmingham, Alabama. Warmer weather is bringing new diseases and new risks to your health. An increase in the number of extreme weather events is starting to make the problem impossible for any of us to ignore—from killer heat waves and devastating droughts to the torrential rains and flash floods that seem to be striking the United States and elsewhere with greater ferocity and frequency as each year passes.

Wherever you live, wherever you go, climate change will find you. The health of you and your family may suffer, and your financial situation certainly will, as these global changes begin to inflict a serious economic burden. The insurance industry alone expects disaster-related costs to rise from a worrying $60 billion each year today to a whopping $300 billion in the coming decades. They have already grown from just $4 billion in the 1950s.

The debate on whether climate change is happening is over. In spite of a handful of vocal skeptics, the evidence is overwhelming, and the scientific community has made up its mind. Climate change has begun, and will continue. There is no doubt about that. With the threat of floods and famines, some fear that a disaster of biblical proportions is inevitable. For those inclined to pessimism, the question now is not *if* this disaster scenario will happen, but *when*.

So is this the beginning of the end?

In truth, it could be, at least to the way of life many of us in the West enjoy. If we continue on our current path, spewing out more and more carbon dioxide and other dangerous gases by the day, then the temperature rise and other changes could leave us feeling very hot under the collar—and burn a huge hole in our wallet, too.

But it is not all bad news. You can make a difference. By taking some of the actions recommended in this book you can help control future greenhouse gas emissions and keep the problem under wraps. While the threat may be global, the solutions will come locally, and all of us must play our part. There is no time to waste; every day we delay merely makes the problem worse.

So it really is up to you. Do nothing, and the doomsayers could be right—it may well be the beginning of the end. Act now, decide to be a part of the solution rather than the problem, and it could be the start of something else, something better. Not the end, perhaps, but a new beginning.

The clock is ticking. It is time to decide.

FURTHER READING AND SOURCES OF INFORMATION

Please note that websites have been referenced wherever possible in order to assist readers who wish to follow up on any particular article, report or book.

INTRODUCTION

BBC, "Global Warming 'Biggest Threat'," January 9, 2004, http://news.bbc.co.uk/2/hi/science/nature/3381425.stm

CNN, "Worst Week of Tornadoes Ends with More Storms," May 10, 2003, http://www.cnn.com/2003/WEATHER/05/10/severe.weather/index.html

Fortune magazine, "The Pentagon's Weather Nightmare," February 9, 2004, http://www.fortune.com/fortune/technology/articles/0,15114,582584,00.html

International Institute for Sustainable Development, *Climate Change Media Reports, 2002–2005,* http://www.iisd.ca/media/climate_atmosphere.htm

The Observer newspaper, "Now the Pentagon Tells Bush: Climate Change Will Destroy Us," February 22, 2004, http://observer.guardian.co.uk/international/story/0,6903,1153513,00.html

World Health Organization, *Climate Change and Human Health—Risks and Responses,* December 2003, http://www.who.int/mediacentre/releases/2003/pr91/en/

World Resources Institute, *Concentrations of Greenhouse Gases and Ozone-depleting Substances, 1744–2001,* 2002, http://earthtrends.wri.org/pdf_library/data_tables/ac3n_2002.PDF

CHAPTER ONE

Earth Policy Institute, *Forest Cover Shrinking,* 2002, http://www.earth-policy.org/Indicators/indicator4.htm

ExxonMobil, "The Outlook for Energy: Energy Beyond 2020," 2003, http://www.exxonmobil.com/corporate/files/corporate/210803.pdf

Sir John Houghton, *Global Warming: The Complete Briefing* (third edition), Cambridge University Press, 2004 (note: this is an excellent resource from one of the world's leading climate scientists who has been a key figure in the Intergovernmental Panel on Climate Change).

Intergovernmental Panel on Climate Change, *Climate Change 2001: The Scientific Basis,* Cambridge University Press, 2001. (Note: this is for those wishing to immerse themselves in the subject in great detail. For the less stout-hearted, you may wish to start with the Summary for Policymakers, which is also available from this website, http://www.grida.no/climate/ipcc_tar/wg1/index.htm)

International Energy Agency, *Key World Energy Statistics,* 2003, http://library.iea.org/dbtw-wpd/Textbase/nppdf/free/2003/key2003.pdf

International Energy Agency, *World Energy Outlook,* 2003, http://www.worldenergyoutlook.org/pubs/index.asp

United Nations Environment Program and GRID Arendal Center (Norway), *Online Briefing Papers on Climate Change,* http://www.grida.no/climate/vital/intro.htm

United Nations Environment Program and World Meteorological Organization, *Common Questions about Climate Change,* hosted on the website of the U.S. Global Change Research Information Office, http://www.gcrio.org/ipcc/qa/index.htm

Union of Concerned Scientists, *Frequently Asked Questions about Global Warming,* http://www.ucsusa.org/global_environment/global_warming/page.cfm?pageID=497

UN Ozone Secretariat, *Information on the Ozone Hole,* 2000, http://www.unep.org/ozone/Public_Information/index.asp

University of Cambridge, *The Ozone Hole Tour,* http://www.atm.ch.cam.ac.uk/tour/

U.S. Environmental Protection Agency's global warming site, http://yosemite.epa.gov/oar/globalwarming.nsf/content/index.html

U.S. Environmental Protection Agency, *Emission Facts,* http://www.epa.gov/otaq/consumer/f00013.htm

U.S. Global Change Research Information Office, *What is Climate Change?* 2004, http://www.gcrio.org/gwcc/part1.html

World Resources Institute, *State of the World 2004: Consumption by the Numbers,* http://www.worldwatch.org/press/news/2004/01/07/

CHAPTER TWO

BBC, "Deadly Hurricane Season," September 28, 2004, http://news.bbc.co.uk/1/hi/world/americas/3677022.stm

CNN, "Hurricane Season 2004 Special Report," October 2004, http://www.cnn.com/SPECIALS/2004/hurricanes/

Environmental News Service, "2003 Third Warmest Year on Record," December 18, 2003, http://www.climateark.org/articles/reader.asp?linkid=27885

Fortune magazine, "The Pentagon's Weather Nightmare," February 9, 2004, http://www.fortune.com/fortune/technology/articles/0,15114,582584,00.html

The Guardian newspaper (London), "US and Oil Lobby Oust Climate Change Scientist," April 20, 2002, http://www.guardian.co.uk/oil/story/0,11319,687649,00.html

Intergovernmental Panel on Climate Change, *Climate Change 2001: The Scientific Basis, Climate Change 2001: The Scientific Basis,* Intergovernmental Panel on Climate Change, Cambridge University Press, 2001 (see in particular the Summary for Policymakers and chapters two, nine and ten), http://www.grida.no/climate/ipcc_tar/wg1/index.htm

International Institute for Sustainable Development, *Climate Change Media Reports, 2002–2005.* Written and compiled by Christopher Spence et al., this website contains an overview of key news stories from major media sources on the science and politics of climate change, http://www.iisd.ca/media/climate_atmosphere.htm

Thomas R. Knutson, National Oceanic and Atmospheric Administration, and Robert E. Tuleya, Center for Coastal Physical Oceanography, Old Dominion University, Virginia, *Impact of CO2-Induced Warming on Simulated Hurricane Intensity and Precipitation: Sensitivity to the Choice of Climate Model and Convective Parameterization,* 2004, http://www.gfdl.noaa.gov/reference/bibliography/2004/tk0401.pdf

The Observer newspaper, "Now the Pentagon Tells Bush: Climate Change Will Destroy Us," February 22, 2004, http://observer.guardian.co.uk/international/story/0,6903,1153513,00.html

Walter A. Robinson of the University of Illinois at Urbana-Champaign, James Hansen of NASA Goddard Institute for Space Studies, and Reto Reudy of Science Systems and Applications, Inc., "The Eastern U.S. Keeps Its Cool," January 18, 2001, http://science.nasa.gov/headlines/y2001/ast18jan_1.htm

U.S. Climate Diagnostics Center, *Climate Change Information,* http://www.cdc.noaa.gov/index.html

U.S. Global Change Research Program, *Climate Change Impacts on the United States, The Potential Consequences of Climate Variability and Change:*

Regional Overview, http://www.usgcrp.gov/usgcrp/Library/nationalassessment/overviewregions.htm

U.S. National Oceanic and Atmospheric Administration, *What Is An El Niño?,* http://www.pmel.noaa.gov/tao/elnino/el-nino-story.html

USA Today, "2004 is 4th Hottest Year for World Since 1861, U.N. Report Says," December 15, 2004, http://www.usatoday.com/weather/news/2004-12-15-hot-year_x.htm

CHAPTER THREE

BBC News online, *Climate Change Information.* The BBC has an excellent, user-friendly website dedicated to information on climate change, particularly its impacts: http://www.bbc.co.uk/climate/

BBC, "Sharp CO2 Rise Divides Opinions," October 11, 2004, http://news.bbc.co.uk/2/hi/science/nature/3732274.stm

Intergovernmental Panel on Climate Change, *Climate Change 2001: Impacts, Adaptation and Vulnerability,* Cambridge University Press, 2001. This second part of the Panel's seminal work, its third and most recent assessment of climate change, deals with its effects on the world around us in great detail, and includes a careful analysis of all major research on the topic involving hundreds of experts. See in particular the Summary for Policymakers and chapters five through ten. http://www.grida.no/climate/ipcc_tar/wg2/index.htm

International Institute for Sustainable Development, *Climate Change Media Reports, 2002–2005.* Written and compiled by Christopher Spence et al., this website contains an overview of key news stories from major media sources on the science and politics of climate change, http://www.iisd.ca/media/climate_atmosphere.htm

Natural Resources Defense Council, *Global Warming.* NRDC offers a website with facts and figures on the effects of climate change on animals and their habitat, http://www.nrdc.org/globalwarming/

Chris Thomas, University of Leeds, et al., "Climate Change Threatens a Million Species with Extinction," January 7, 2004, http://www.leeds.ac.uk/media/current/extinction.htm

UN Environment Program, "Dead Zones Emerging as Big Threat to 21st Century Fish Stocks," March 28, 2004, http://www.unep.org/Documents.Multilingual/Default.asp?DocumentID=388&ArticleID=4458&l=en

WWF, *The Implications of Climate Change for Australia's Great Barrier Reef,* 2004. Written by Hans Hoegh-Guldberg and Ove Hoegh-Guldberg and published by conservation group WWF, this report considers the impact of global warming on coral reefs, http://www.wwf.org.au/News_and_information/News_room/viewnews.php?news_id=65

WWF, *Turning up the Heat: How Global Warming Threatens Life in the Sea,* 1999. Amy Mathews-Amos and Ewann A. Berntson, Marine Conservation Biology Institute, Seattle, wrote this article for conservation group WWF, http://www.panda.org/news_facts/newsroom/news.cfm?uNewsId= 1958&uLangId=1

CHAPTER FOUR

BBC, "Deaths from Heatstroke 'Set to Double'," November 22, 2000, http://news.bbc.co.uk/1/hi/sci/tech/1034598.stm

Intergovernmental Panel on Climate Change, *Climate Change 2001: Impacts, Adaptation and Vulnerability,* Cambridge University Press, 2001. (Background information: Six hundred experts from more than 80 countries contributed to this report from the Intergovernmental Panel on Climate Change, the most authoritative international source of expertise on global warming. The full report, which runs to about 1,000 pages and took 3 years to complete, contains detailed information on the impacts of climate change, compiling and reviewing information and research from literally thousands of studies and reports. The report includes sections outlining impacts in each region [North America is covered in chapter 15.]) It can be downloaded section-by-section from: http://www.grida.no/climate/ipcc_tar/wg2/index.htm)

International Institute for Sustainable Development, *Climate Change Media Reports, 2002–2005.* Written and compiled by Christopher Spence et al., this website contains an overview of key news stories from major media sources on the science and politics of climate change, http://www.iisd.ca/media/climate_atmosphere.htm

Munich Re, "2004 Costliest Natural Disaster Year Ever for Insurance Industry, Weather Extremes a Result of Global Warming," http://www.munichre.com/default_e.asp (Press/Media section)

Munich Re, "Munich Re's Analysis of Natural Catastrophes in 2003: Economic and Insured Losses Continue to Increase at a High Level," December 29, 2003, http://www.munichre.com/default_e.asp (Press/Media section)

U.S. Centers for Disease Control and Prevention website. The CDC provides detailed, up-to-date information about many of the potential health risks associated with global warming, http://www.cdc.gov

U.S. Energy Information Administration, *Emissions of Greenhouse Gases in the United States 2003,* December 2004, ftp://ftp.eia.doe.gov/pub/oiaf/1605/cdrom/pdf/ggrpt/057303.pdf

U.S. Environmental Protection Agency website briefings, http://yosemite.epa.gov/oar/globalwarming.nsf/

World Resources Institute, "WRI warns global warming endangers future Winter Olympics," February 18, 2002, http://climate.wri.org/news-release_text.cfm?NewsReleaseID=22

CHAPTER FIVE

Carbon Group, *Carbon Down, Profits Up*, 2004, http://www.theclimate-group.org/370.php

Ross Gelbspan, *Boiling Point (How Politicians, Big Oil and Coal, Journalists, and Activists Have Fueled the Climate Crisis—and What We Can Do to Avert Disaster)*, Basic Books, 2004.

International Institute for Sustainable Development, *Climate Change Media Reports, 2002–2005*. Written and compiled by Christopher Spence et al., this website contains an overview of key news stories from major media sources on the science and politics of climate change, http://www.iisd.ca/media/climate_atmosphere.htm

Kyoto Protocol, 1997. The complete text of the Kyoto Protocol to the UN Climate Change Convention is available online at: http://unfccc.int/resource/docs/convkp/kpeng.pdf

Natural Resources Defense Council, "The Cheney Energy Task Force: A Review and Analysis of the Proceedings Leading to the Bush Administration's Formulation of its May 2001 Energy Policy," April 2004, http://www.nrdc.org/globalwarming

UN Climate Change Secretariat, *Caring for Climate: A Guide to the Climate Change Convention and the Kyoto Protocol*, 2003. This guide to climate change and the international response to the problem can be downloaded from: http://unfccc.int/resource/cfc_guide.pdf

UN Climate Change Secretariat, *A Guide to the Climate Change Convention Process*, 2002. This guide explains how the Climate Change Convention works. To read it, visit: http://unfccc.int/resource/process/guideprocess-p.pdf

UN Environment Program and UN Climate Change Secretariat, *Understanding Climate Change: A Beginner's Guide to the UN Framework Convention and its Kyoto Protocol*, 2002. This user-friendly introduction to the UN climate change treaty and Kyoto Protocol is available online at: http://unfccc.int/resource/beginner_02_en.pdf

United Nations Framework Convention on Climate Change, 1992. The complete text of the UN climate treaty is available online at: http://unfccc.int/resource/docs/convkp/conveng.pdf

White House Report, *Current U.S. Actions to Address Climate Change,* 2002, www.whitehouse.gov/news/releases/2001/06/climatechange.pdf

CHAPTER SIX

Business Week magazine, "Global Warming: Consensus is Growing Among Scientists, Governments, and Business that They Must Act Fast to Combat Climate Change," August 16, 2004.

Center for Public Integrity, "Big Oil Protects its Interests: Industry spends hundreds of millions on lobbying, elections," July 15, 2004, http://www.publicintegrity.org/oil/report.aspx?aid=345

Friends of the Earth International, "Litigation Warms Up Climate Talks," December 14, 2004, http://www.foei.org/media/2004/1214.html

Ross Gelbspan, *Boiling Point (How Politicians, Big Oil and Coal, Journalists, and Activists Have Fueled the Climate Crisis—and What We Can Do to Avert Disaster),* Basic Books, 2004.

Ross Gelbspan, *The Heat Is On: The Climate Crisis, the Cover-Up, the Prescription,* Basic Books, 1997.

International Institute for Sustainable Development, *Climate Change Media Reports, 2002–2005.* Written and compiled by Christopher Spence et al., this website contains an overview of key news stories from major media sources on the science and politics of climate change, http://www.iisd.ca/media/climate_atmosphere.htm

New Statesman newspaper, George Marshall and Mark Lynas, "Why We Don't Give a Damn," November 2003

New York Times, Danny Hakim, "Catching Up to the Cost of Global Warming," July 25, 2004, www.nytimes.com/2004/07/25/business/your-money/25warm.html?ex=10920415

Pew Center, Climate Change briefing papers, 2004. The Pew Center on Global Climate Change, a major think tank based in Washington, D.C., offers many reports and insights into the climate change issue, particularly as it affects the United States: www.pewclimate.org

U.S. Climate Change Science Program, *Our Changing Planet. The U.S. Climate Change Science Program for Fiscal Years 2004 and 2005,* August 2004, http://www.usgcrp.gov/usgcrp/Library/ocp2004-5/default.htm

WWF, "New Climate Change Report To Congress Should Spur Action," August 26, 2004, http://www.worldwildlife.org/news/displayPR.cfm?prID=137

CHAPTER SEVEN

The American Council for an Energy-Efficient Economy provides an easy-to-use guide to the most energy efficient appliances: www.aceee.org/consumerguide.

The Energy Guide site (www.energyguide.com) provides extensive information on energy efficiency and your home's energy use.

Jeffrey Langholz and Kelly Turner, *You Can Prevent Global Warming (and Save Money!)*, Andrews McMeel Publishing, 2003. This informative and detailed book presents 51 different ways you can help combat global warming while also saving over $2,000 a year.

The League of Conservation Voters—or LCV—is a nonprofit group dedicated to promoting pro-environment policies in Congress and the White House. The LCV's website rates every member of Congress and the administration so you can decide which deserves your support. Visit: www.lcv.org/scorecard.

The U.S. Department of Energy's Office of Energy Efficiency and Renewable Energy offers many tips to help cut your electricity bills around the home. Visit: www.eere.energy.gov/consumerinfo/energy_savers/.

U.S Energy Star system. The U.S. government has set up an energy rating system that will tell you which models are best. It's called Energy Star. For more information, visit: www.energystar.gov.

Index

DATE DUE